# INVENTING
# JOY

## Dare to Build a Brave & Creative Life

## JOY MANGANO

WITH ALEX TRESNIOWSKI

SIMON & SCHUSTER

NEW YORK   LONDON   TORONTO   SYDNEY   NEW DELHI

Simon & Schuster
1230 Avenue of the Americas
New York, NY 10020

First Simon & Schuster hardcover edition November 2017

SIMON & SCHUSTER and colophon are registered
trademarks of Simon & Schuster, Inc.

For information about special discounts for bulk purchases,
please contact Simon & Schuster Special Sales at
1-866-506-1949 or business@simonandschuster.com.

The Simon & Schuster Speakers Bureau can bring authors to your live event.
For more information or to book an event, contact the
Simon & Schuster Speakers Bureau at 1-866-248-3049
or visit our website at www.simonspeakers.com.

*Interior design by Ruth Lee-Mui*
*Cover photo makeup by D'Angelo Thompson*
*Cover photo hairstyling by Mordechai Alvow*

Manufactured in the United States of America

1   3   5   7   9   10   8   6   4   2

Library of Congress Cataloging-in-Publication Data is available.

ISBN 978-1-5011-7620-3
ISBN 978-1-5011-7621-0 (ebook)

*For all the dreamers in the world.*

# PART
# ONE

*"NO MATTER WHO YOU ARE*
*OR WHERE YOU'RE FROM,*
*YOU HAVE THE POWER TO CHANGE THE WORLD."*

JOY MANGANO

# 1

One night when I was ten years old, I saved my dog, Duke.

It was the middle of winter, and I was sitting in my parents' bedroom trying to block out the sounds coming from downstairs. My parents were arguing about something again, and I just wanted a quiet place to sit and be alone. Anyway, I looked out the window and saw Duke, our beautiful black German shepherd, in the backyard. Duke could sometimes be grumpy with strangers, but he was always a sweet little puppy dog with me. In the backyard, our small in-ground pool had frozen over, and Duke was walking on the ice.

Suddenly the ice cracked, and Duke fell through.

No one noticed but me. My parents were too busy downstairs, and my brother, John, was in his room. I ran out the back door and found Duke scratching at the edge of the pool, trying desperately to get out. I was small for my age, and I was skinny as a stick—I used to wear thermal underwear under my clothes just so I wouldn't look like I was starving—but still I found the strength to grab on to Duke's paws and pull him out of the water. He was shivering, and all four of his paws were cut and bleeding from scratching against the side of the pool.

I took Duke inside and wrapped him in a towel, and I put some bandages on his paws, and I sat with him and held him until he warmed up and calmed down.

Over the next two days I changed Duke's bandages four times. It was hard, messy work, and probably kind of painful for Duke. He didn't like it, and neither did I. And when I was changing them for the fourth time, a thought formed in my head.

*There has to be a better way.*

So I came up with an idea for these special bandage booties for Duke. The outsides of the booties were like socks, but on the insides I layered gauze pads that I could just take out and replace. I'd slip them on Duke and pull them tight, and that would be that. At first, Duke didn't know what to make of the booties, and he'd sort of clomp around in them and look at me as if to say, *Are you kidding me with this?* But after a while he got used to them and didn't seem to mind. I remember seeing him walk by in his little booties and thinking he looked so cute.

I also remember thinking, *Okay, they work. The crazy booties work. This is better.*

Fast-forward thirty years.

I was on vacation with my three young children, Christie, Bobby, and Jackie, in East Hampton on Long Island. One afternoon, the children and I were sitting on a bench outside a bakery on Main Street, eating ice cream. I watched as a man came out of the store holding two white cardboard pie boxes, one in each hand.

The man tried to push the screen door open with his elbows, but it kept swinging back and nearly knocking the boxes out of his hands. Finally, he escaped the store. As he walked to his car, he stacked one box on top of the other and balanced them with one hand while digging around in his pocket for his keys. He got them out but dropped them on the sidewalk. Somehow, he recovered and made it into his car with his two pies still intact. It was a little adventure no one paid any attention to but me.

And as I watched the man struggle with his pies, a thought formed in my head again. The exact same thought as when I was ten.

*There has to be a better way.*

And in that very moment, I saw it. Clear as day.

As a mom, I baked a lot of cupcakes for my children's birthday parties and school events, and the only thing big enough to carry twenty-four cupcakes was a flimsy cardboard shirt box. I'd put cellophane or tinfoil on top of the cupcakes, but inevitably the icing would get smushed.

But what if . . . what if . . .

. . . what if there was a box specially designed for the job?

Something with, say, six sides and a little shelf that gave you two separate layers for pies or all twenty-four cupcakes? And maybe the shelf could come out and you'd have enough room for a triple-layer cake! And what if the bottom popped up so the box folded up flat for easy storage, unlike those big plastic tubs that take up all the room in your cabinets? And what if it made life easier for moms everywhere who were constantly baking cakes and cookies and pies for school events and birthday parties and could never really figure out how to carry them?

Why couldn't such a box exist?

I grabbed the kids and rushed back to where we were staying. I found some paper and started scribbling drawings of the box. I spent the whole day reworking and refining the design. I saw the entire process in my head: how I could make them, what they'd be made of, the many ways they could help out mothers like me—everything. It was all there, in the air, waiting for me to pluck it out.

Just about sixteen months later, the Piatto Bakery Box was born—and it went on to become one of the most popular products of its kind, ever.

That moment outside the bakery was an epiphany for me. It was the moment when I realized—truly realized—what I was really good at. You see, other people in the store and on the sidewalk saw the man struggling with his pies, but no one paid him any attention. No one saw what I saw. As far as I could tell, no one viewed the situation quite the way I did—oh, there's a problem, so what's the solution? But for whatever reason, I did see it that way. It was just the way my mind worked in that instant. And it made me realize, like I never really had before, that this is who I am, and this was what I do.

I see objects that aren't there.

I solve problems no one asks me to solve.

I look at life in terms of meaningful, positive, impactful change, even if it's just a better pie box.

I'm an inventor, and I make things.

This is the part of the book where I'm supposed to tell you about all the things I've made and everything I've accomplished. Some of you may already know parts of my story, but many of you might not, so the idea is to set up who I am and give you a reason to keep reading. To be honest, I'm not really thrilled about this part. How do you write about your successes without sounding like you're bragging?

Some people get someone else to do it in a prologue or a foreword—someone notable who can get away with singing your praises to the heavens. But I didn't want to do that, either.

I want this entire book, start to finish, to be like a conversation between you and me. Like you're sitting with a friend, feet up on the sofa, listening to her tell a story.

My whole life and career have been about having direct and heartfelt connections with the people who cross my path and grace me with their trust and attention. I've spent thousands of hours on TV addressing hundreds of millions of people, and in all that time I've done one thing and one thing only—spoken straight from my heart.

I want this book to be the same way. Just me, talking to you, straight from my heart.

So here goes.

My name is Joy, and I grew up in a working-class part of Long Island in New York. My father ran a bus company, and my mother took care of me and my brother, John. Things weren't always perfect in our house, but they weren't always bad, either. Growing up, I was insecure and not very popular. I can't say I was a quiet person, but I definitely wasn't flashy.

The people around me, though—they *were* flashy. My father, Rudy, who drove big lime-green cars and wore white boat shoes, and my mother, Toots, who liked to wear big stylish hats everywhere, and later on my husband, Tony, an aspiring singer and life of the party who wasn't really ready to be a father to our three children.

In my thirties I felt like I was losing control of my life, so I took charge and made some changes, and I rediscovered who I could be.

Then I invented the first self-wringing mop, and that changed everything.

I called it the Miracle Mop, and in the early days my children and friends and family helped me build the first 1,000 of them out of the back of my father's auto body shop in Deer Park, Long Island.

I convinced someone at QVC, a new electronic retail TV channel, to sell the Miracle Mop. And despite having zero TV experience—and a terrible fear of public speaking—I wound up on the air selling the mops myself.

Not too much later, we were selling millions of Miracle Mops a year.

How did I do it? How did I sell so many mops on TV?

I did it by talking straight from my heart.

After the Miracle Mop, I just kept seeing things that weren't there. I came up with the idea for a better, slimmer, more efficient closet hanger, which struck most people as an unnecessary solution to a nonexistent problem. A hanger is just a hanger, they said. Who cares about hangers? Well, I did, and so did a lot of other people with messy, overstuffed closets and nice clothes that kept ending up on the floor.

I launched the Huggable Hanger on the Home Shopping Network, and it became the single best-selling product in the history of HSN—and all of TV.

More products followed, and more successes, and nearly all of my inventions earned the Good Housekeeping Seal, my own personal benchmark for quality. *Fast Company* magazine named me one of the 10 Most Creative Women in Business, and *People* magazine called me The Billion-Dollar Mom. Each year my appearances on the shopping channel HSN are beamed into more than 90 million homes.

All told, I've designed and invented more than $3 billion worth of products, all of them for people just like me.

Still, my proudest achievement, besides my three beautiful children, is the little company I started back in 1991, Ingenious Designs. It grew big enough for me to employ more than 200 people, including two of my children (who aren't children anymore, and who gave up impressive careers of their own to come work with me). My mother, Toots, and my father, Rudy, also came to work with me, even after they were divorced (I *did* have to put them in different parts of the building). Over the years, other friends and family came on board, including, believe it or not, my ex-husband, Tony.

I guess I look at the concept of family a little differently than some people. I believe that just because bad things happen in relationships doesn't mean there isn't something worth saving there. I believe in circling back to people and seeing the good in them instead of the bad.

Yes, I'm an inventor, and, yes, I've sold a lot of products and won awards and all that, but if you want to know what matters most to me— what makes me *me*—it's family.

So if you share my belief in the power of ideas and dreams and family, I hope you'll keep on reading.

I believe we are all capable of great creativity and great productivity and great achievement in our lives. I believe we can all make meaningful, impactful changes that will make the world around us better. We all have unique tools and talents and abilities that, when deployed with true passion and purpose and courage, can produce astonishing, magical results.

I believe these things because I see how far I've come with my own set of tools and talents and abilities—and it's a lot farther than I ever dreamed I could go.

Which brings me to the reason why I decided to write this book in the first place.

You see, it's been a long and incredible journey for me, from skinny little Joy to single mother of three to the great here and now. And through it all, I managed to defy a lot of conventional wisdom, and I developed my own set of truths. Today, these truths are my core principles—they are what I live by each and every day, in every aspect of my life.

And any one of them, on its own, can help you make a meaningful change in your life.

But taken together, they form a kind of guide that I use to make positive changes in the world around me. I call it my Blueprint.

My Blueprint for a more joyful life.

And that's what this book is about.

So, technically, this book is not a memoir or an autobiography, although it does tell the story of my life.

And, technically, it's not a self-help book, either, though I certainly hope it proves helpful.

To me, this book is a shared moment between me and you. As I tell you my stories, I want you to feel like you're right there with me, facing the same obstacles, figuring out solutions, taking the journey with me.

Along the way, I'll pause in my story, but only when there's something really important I want to point out to you. It won't happen in every chapter, but close to it. I'll even use a little light bulb—💡—to help mark these moments. Because I want you to learn what I learned, exactly when I learned it.

And in the end, after all the stories are told, we'll come back around to my Blueprint. We'll walk through it together, and we'll see if some of it might help you build your own brave and creative life.

I believe it will.

I know with all my heart that you can carve a beautiful, joyful path through the world. And I hope my story can inspire and empower you as you take on the most courageous task of all.

Inventing *you*.

# 2

Before we jump in, I just wanted to throw an idea out there for you to think about.

The idea that Everything Is a Product.

I know that might sound a little crass, but that's not how I mean it. For me, it's just the way my mind works. It's a big part of how I view my life, and how I view the world around me. I see everything as a product— and I mean everything.

And it always seems to lead me to a little bit of magic.

Let me tell you what I mean.

I often hear people say that my instincts for designing and creating things amount to some kind of superpower. As in, "Oh, that's Joy's superpower—she just knows what works and what doesn't." It's a nice compliment to hear and it always makes me smile, but you know what?

It's not true.

The truth is, there is nothing superhuman about me. Trust me, there isn't. I'm thoroughly human, and I have all the fears and doubts and insecurities that come with being human. I get upset when bad things happen and happy when things go right. I'm not off the charts in any department, and I'm certainly not brilliant (I know people who are brilliant, and I'm not like them). In most ways, I'm pretty normal. What you see is what you get.

But what I do have going for me, and what has propelled me to where I am today, is something that is incredibly simple and powerful all at once: I believe in my ideas, and I have the courage to act on them.

When I see something that isn't working right in my life, I believe I have the option, even the responsibility, to say something and do something about it. I feel confident that my voice matters, that I can fix what's broken and make it better—even if it's just a little bit.

I don't feel this way because I am special.

I feel this way because, like everyone else, I have the right—and the power—to make my life work better.

Sometimes we forget we have this power. We begin to believe our voices don't matter. We accept that we're not in control of our lives, so why should we even bother trying to fix things? So here's a little trick I use to remind myself that I *do* have this power, and that my voice *does* matter.

I think of myself as a consumer, and I think of everything around me as a product. As a consumer, I have the right to speak up about what's working and what's not.

We can all understand how a can opener is a product. And we can tell when a can opener isn't working, because it just isn't opening any cans. Wouldn't you feel *very* confident in your opinion that the can opener is broken? That it's not doing what it's supposed to do? That it needs fixing?

Well, what if you're a parent, and your son or daughter is mad at you and won't let you into their room?

Would you say, *Oh, well, teenagers are teenagers, and there's nothing I can do about it?*

Or would you say, *Wait a minute, this isn't working right, I need to fix it right now?*

Would you speak up about a can opener, but not do the same with your child?

Everything can be a product. Your job. Your relationships. Your family. Everything. The beauty of viewing everything as a product is that it expands the range of subjects we feel entitled to have an opinion on. It empowers us to have more influence in our own lives. Because if you are the consumer of everything in your life, then *you are entitled to a point of view about how the "products" actually work.*

Who better than us to evaluate whether something is working the way we want it to? If our voices don't matter, then whose do?

In my business, some people believe they're smarter than the consumers they service. But I never, ever make that mistake. I know the smartest person in any transaction is *always* the consumer, because they have all the power in their hands. They decide what they want and what they don't want. The consumer is the real expert.

That is true in business, and it's *especially* true in the business of life.

We are the ultimate arbiters, the ultimate experts, of what works and doesn't work in our worlds.

Some people shy away from this responsibility because they're afraid they'll be criticized or ridiculed if they make their voice heard.

But we shouldn't shy away. We shouldn't be afraid. If something isn't working in our lives, it will never get fixed unless we admit to ourselves that it's broken—and find the courage to fix it.

So go ahead and try it for a while—think of everything as a product. Think of yourself as the consumer of that product, and have the courage to believe that your opinion, your point of view, your voice, really and truly matters in the transactions that make up your life.

If we're confident we can tell when a can opener is broken, let's be the same way with the things that really matter in our lives.

# 3

My father, Rudy, was in the front seat, driving his big white Cadillac home from a winter vacation in Vermont. My mother, Toots, who was wearing one of the big hats she loved so much, was in the passenger seat. I was in back, squeezed in next to my older brother, John, my grandmother Mimi, and five or six of my mother's giant hat boxes (she always traveled with extras).

It was a long drive, and every few minutes Mimi whispered something in my ear.

"Do you think he's going to stop soon?" she said. "I need to go to the bathroom."

Mimi never really got along with Rudy. Maybe she didn't think he was good enough for her daughter. In any case, she didn't want to ask him to stop. After a while I felt sorry for her and finally spoke up.

"Dad, Mimi needs to go to the bathroom!"

My father said he'd pull over. Then he told my mother his lips were chapped and asked if she had any lip balm.

"All I have is this," Toots said, holding up a tube of bright gold lipstick.

Rudy took the lipstick and put it on.

A few minutes later he pulled into a gas station in the middle of nowhere, and a burly attendant came over to the car. My dad rolled down the window. I looked at the attendant's confused face as he surveyed the scene—Mimi squirming in the back, me and John buried under boxes, Toots wearing her big fancy hat, and my father wearing bright gold lipstick.

"Do you have a ladies' room?" my father asked.

Welcome to my family.

Looking back, I think it's fair to say my parents were on the eccentric side.

Rudy and Toots—her real name is Terry, but everyone calls her Toots—met at a bridal shower in Brooklyn, where Rudy grew up. His parents came over from Italy, where they'd been forced into an arranged marriage. I didn't know his parents all that well, but from what people said, they weren't the happiest people around. They had seven children in all, and Rudy was in the middle. Rudy's father was known to be mean to his children, and especially to Rudy, who he constantly called the black sheep of the family.

Toots's parents were different. Her father, Pappy, was a printer, and her mother, Mimi, had a job as a waitress during the Depression. Mimi was such a hard worker but she was always positive and full of energy, and so much fun to be with. Toots was their only child, and she was loved and cherished and doted on, and I think that shaped the rest of her life. As an adult she always wanted to be the beautiful object of attention, and she loved shopping for fashionable outfits and hats, even when we couldn't really afford it.

One time she came home with a two-foot-tall beehive hairdo, which made it kind of hard for her to put on her stylish hats.

Rudy was eccentric in a different way. After dropping out of high school, he got a job driving a bus, and eventually started his own bus company on Long Island. That was how he supported his family, and it was a perfectly good job.

Still, not having a real education bothered him more than it probably should have. It didn't help that his father harped on him for being a dropout. Rudy made up for it by reading lots of books and acting like an authority on a wide, and sometimes weird, range of subjects—turtle species in the Galápagos Islands, antique grandfather clocks, you name it. He always wanted to be smarter than everyone else, even people who clearly knew more about something than he did.

Like Toots, Rudy also had a flair for the dramatic. He liked wearing smart dinner jackets and slick white shoes, and he loved driving flashy cars that came in wild colors. When my mother said she wanted a pink car, Rudy bought her a tiny pink Fiat. It was so small, one neighbor said that if she drove over a piece of gum, she'd stick to it.

To be closer to his bus company, Rudy and Toots moved from Brooklyn to a three-bedroom colonial home in Dix Hills, a middle-class hamlet in the town of Huntington, right in the middle of Long Island. They had a son, my brother John, and three years later I came along.

Skinny little Joy.

I was born with a hernia and clogged tear ducts, and when my baby teeth came in they were fragile and already falling apart. As a child I wore braces and big glasses and clothes that looked too large for me. I remember wanting to be the kind of girl who people fussed over and pinched on the cheek and told, "Oh, aren't you a pretty child!" I remember wanting to be as beautiful as my mother. But I just wasn't. I was skinny and self-conscious and awkward. In the third grade I still wore braces and big glasses, and my eyes constantly watered because of my tear ducts, and I think my teacher, Miss Haffercamp, felt sorry for me, because one day she came over and patted me on the shoulder and gave me a little pep talk.

"Joy, it's okay," she said. "Don't you know how special you are? Everything's going to be okay."

A few weeks later, Miss Haffercamp began casting the annual school play. That year, it was *Peter Pan*. I *loved Peter Pan*. My parents had a vinyl recording of a production of the show, and in my room I played it about a thousand times, acting out all the parts myself. I was secretly hoping Miss Haffercamp would give me a tiny role in the play—something that would let me be onstage but behind everyone else.

Instead, she asked me if I wanted to try out for the lead role—Peter Pan.

I didn't want to do it. I didn't want to be front and center. Just the thought of it was terrifying. But when Miss Haffercamp asked me, I said yes. Maybe it was because she was so nice to me. I went to the audition and got the part, and I played Peter Pan in front of an auditorium full of parents and teachers. I was petrified the whole time, but I got through it.

I can't say that moment changed my life, because it didn't. It took me a long, long time to believe in myself the way Miss Haffercamp believed in me. Much longer than you might think.

But Miss Haffercamp's kindness made a real difference.

# 4

One day when I was eight years old, my mother took me with her to the supermarket. Near the checkout line, I noticed another girl around my age standing next to a giant display tower of canned peas. The girl reached out and touched one of the cans, and all of a sudden—BANG!

The tower came tumbling down with a giant crash.

Everyone turned and stared at the girl, including her mother, who looked really mad. I could tell the girl herself was just a couple of seconds away from crying.

Without thinking about it, I rushed over to the girl and the sprawling mess of cans. "Don't worry," I told her. "I'll help you put them back."

And that's what I did. Together, we started restacking the cans. Later on, my mother told me how, when the cans came down, my own face reflected a kind of horror, as if I'd been the one to knock them over—which, in a way, is what it felt like to me. I mean, I could really feel the girl's fear and embarrassment when everyone was staring at her. My instinct was to go to her so she wouldn't be alone, and to help her so people would stop staring.

That wasn't the only time I felt like that. In Dix Hills, I had a cousin named Phil who lived down the street. Phil was a sweet and funny kid, but because he was smaller than other boys his age, he got picked on a lot. The boys called him names and chased him around the playground and harassed him on the school bus. I hated it when I saw kids being mean to Phil.

At school one afternoon, I saw some boys circling Phil in the playground. I knew what was coming next. I ran toward them, my hands balled into tiny fists, and I stood in front of Phil and faced the boys.

"You are NOT messing with Phil today!" I screamed.

The boys got quiet. They looked at each other, not sure what to do. Then they shrugged and walked away. I don't know how I did it, but somehow I projected enough authority to scare the bullies away. Seeing Phil get picked on—seeing *anyone* get picked on—hurt me as much as if I were the one being bullied.

My father Rudy had a temper, and when he got frustrated or annoyed or angry he might yell and kick over a chair, or throw a dinner plate against the wall. I always wanted my mother to stand up to him, but she never did.

Rudy was tougher on my brother, John, than he was with me. When he got mad at John for whatever reason, he might chase him around the house with a strap. Not often, but often enough to matter. I did what I could to protect John, but I couldn't save him every time.

Rudy never hit me, though one time he came close. It happened at the kitchen table, when he got angry about something. I was almost nine, and I remember being annoyed by his temper, so I got up and grabbed a box of chocolate snaps that was on the table, and I stormed away, headed to my bedroom. Then I heard my father's angry voice.

"Give me those chocolate snaps," he said.

I kept going, but my father reached out and grabbed the box out of my hands. He put the box up against the wall, right next to where my head was. Then he punched the box with his fist, shattering everything in it.

The kitchen got quiet. My mother and brother said nothing. I looked at my father, and he looked at me. I knew he had crushed the snaps so I couldn't eat them, but I also knew he was trying to make a point.

He was saying, *I am someone. Do not challenge me.*

Part of me wanted to cry and run off to my bedroom, but that's not what I did. Instead, I got angry. I looked right at my father and let him have it.

"Don't you *dare* ever do that again," I said.

*Then* I stormed off to my room.

I wasn't just standing up for myself. I was standing up for my mother and my brother, too.

My father spent the next three days apologizing to me for his outburst. It might have scared him how close he came to hitting me. Or maybe the fact that I stood up to him was the scary part. Either way, our relationship changed that day.

I didn't know it then, but what I was feeling in all of those moments was empathy. The ability to understand and share the emotions of others. Empathy is something most of us possess and demonstrate every day. We help people when they trip and fall. We feel bad when we hear about some-one's misfortune. It's part of what makes us human.

With me, feeling what someone else was feeling also made me want to do something about it. It made me want to find a way to make things better. My impulse was to step in and fix what was broken.

Looking back now, I realize that my ability to empathize with others shaped the person I would become—and led directly to my success as an inventor. And I've seen the same ability drive the success of others.

I believe the key to success is how deeply we care about, and how closely we identify with, the people around us.

When I create a product, I'm not observing consumers and trying to figure out what they need, as if they're separate from me. I feel what they feel, and I need what they need. It's not part of a business strategy or even anything I set out to do. It's just who I am—the same person who felt the embarrassment of the little girl who knocked over the peas.

This connection is essential not only in business but in all facets of life. To accomplish anything meaningful in any endeavor, we have to un-derstand the value of what we are doing not just for ourselves but *for other people.*

Think about it—it's hard to solve any problem if we're seeing only one side of it. If we're arguing with a friend, we won't be able to fix what's broken unless we empathize with them and understand their needs, not just our own. *Empathy is absolutely crucial to success.*

Now here's the good news—the ability to empathize is already inside us. It's part of our internal wiring. What we need to do is harness that power. We need to listen to the caring voice inside us and pull that em-pathy to the surface.

This is one of the most important lessons I've learned—that to be truly successful in anything, we need to turn our focus outward and tune in to other people's emotions. Only then can we try to fix what's broken.

# 5

I was nine years old when I ran away from home.

I was angry with my mother about something, I can't even remember what, but it was enough for me to decide to take Kim, the German shepherd we had before Duke, and just walk out.

But before I did, I went to the backyard and found the straightest, most perfect stick I could find, and I meticulously tied a scarf to one end of it, knotting it neatly in two places so it made the perfect little carrying case—just like those bags on a stick that hoboes always had, only more efficient. I packed a few things in it for me, and also some food for Kim, and I put her on a leash, and we walked out the front door, never to return.

About thirty seconds later, my mother got a phone call from a neighbor.

"Joy's out here with a dog and a stick."

My mother got in her car, drove down the street and found us and brought us home. All I will say is it wasn't just a stick.

It was my beautiful and perfect little creation.

Like a lot of kids, I loved finding ways to create new things to play with. I guess I just took it to a whole other level.

For instance, I loved playing with dolls, but the dolls were secondary to what was really fun for me—creating elaborate cities for my dolls to live in. I'd make buildings out of cardboard, and little streets and sidewalks, and I could fill up my whole bedroom with my doll cities.

One day, my brother announced that he and some of his neighborhood friends were going to build a treehouse. I told John I wanted to help. I got out some sketch paper and designed a treehouse that had not one, not two, but *seven* levels. With the help of the man who was working with my father to put up a deck, John and I lugged slats of wood across the yard and hammered them together ourselves, and in the end our treehouse was unlike any we'd ever seen. It really *was* seven levels!

Then I turned my attention to the kitchen.

My family had an ordinary toaster oven we used to heat up waffles and things like that. But what I wanted to do was roast pumpkin seeds and make them pop. Our toaster oven simply couldn't generate that much heat. Then I had an idea.

I was smart enough not to mess with the toaster's wiring. But I did line the inside of the toaster with aluminum foil, thinking the heat would bounce off the foil and roast the seeds more thoroughly. I didn't ask my parents for permission to fool around with the toaster, in case you're wondering.

Once I'd completely lined the little oven with tinfoil, I put in the pumpkin seeds and turned it on.

Immediately, it caught on fire and began smoking, and after a few seconds it fizzled out. I guess I'm lucky I didn't get killed. But for sure I killed our family's toaster oven.

The best thing about little Joy the inventor was that she didn't think she had to be really good at something in order to give it a try.

And you know what? She was right.

When we're children, we tend to believe we can do anything. Never built a treehouse? So what? Lit the toaster on fire? Close call! We seem to be born with a type of fearless creativity—we have ideas, and we aren't afraid to take a chance or two to bring them to life. And if we make mistakes and mess things up, that's okay, because that's how we learn what works and what doesn't.

But as we grow older, we tend to shut this fearlessness off. We are taught that being skeptical is smart, and we become our own worst critic. We allow our fear of not succeeding, of not being good, of being embarrassed or feeling lost, to stop us from even trying in the first place.

And *that's* the real mistake.

Our smart, skeptical adult selves shut down ideas for something new. Even good ideas. *Especially* good ideas, because those are the ones that feel more real, more tempting, more frightening. We do this because we forget what we once took for granted as children—that we probably won't be any good at something the first time we try it.

We forget that we don't have to be good to get started. We just have to get started.

When I was nine, I wasn't afraid to create something new. And I wasn't worried about it working or not. I did my best, and sometimes it worked, and sometimes it didn't. Sometimes it caught on fire.

My brother would always say to me, "You should have been born a boy." I understood what he meant—that boys build things like rocket ships, not girls.

But what can I say? I just wanted to build rocket ships.

# 6

"Joy, I'm having a party this weekend, do you want to come?"

I was in junior high, and one of my classmates was inviting me to her home. She said all the other girls from our class would be there, and lots of boys, too. I knew what that meant. It meant they'd be playing games like spin the bottle.

"I'd like to, but I can't," I lied. "I'm going away with my parents."

I was just too insecure to have the nerve to go to parties with all the popular kids. I wanted to go—I wanted to be one of the popular girls. Believe me, if I could have closed my eyes and made a wish and turned myself into a pretty, confident cheerleader, I would have. But I couldn't. That just wasn't me. Over time, all my friends had boyfriends, but I didn't. Not for the longest time.

Instead, I went in the opposite direction and buried myself in school-work. I was part of the National Junior Honor Society and the Girls

Leadership program. I was a teacher's aide, and I was in all the honors classes I could take. I also tried out for all the sports teams—hockey, gymnastics, basketball, softball, volleyball—and I was even voted team captain.

At school, we had several buses that took students home after classes, and the last one—the one for kids who had sports or other extracurricular activities—left at 6:00 p.m.

I was *always* on the 6:00 p.m. bus.

There were only two places where I felt like I really belonged. One of them was at school. And the other was on a pair of skis.

From the very first time I skied—when I was five and our parents took John and me to a snowy little mountain in upstate New York—I was in love with it. Growing up I'd ski every chance I got, even on school trips. I got better and better, and by the time I was approaching high school I was an expert skier. I decided I was good enough to maybe become an Olympic skier, and maybe even win a gold medal.

My brother, John, was a skier, too, and before applying to college he enrolled for a year in the Stowe Preparatory School in Vermont. Stowe was a unique school that allowed students to build their curriculums around skiing. When I was fourteen I decided I wanted to go there, too.

So I marched into the living room and told my parents, "I'm going to be a skier and I'm going to Stowe, and that's what I'm going to do."

"Sorry, Joy, you can't," my father said.

The first problem was the tuition—my parents couldn't really afford it. But that wasn't the only issue. To get into Stowe, you had to take a three-week-long, 300-mile hike through upstate New York and into Vermont, a journey that included a three-day solo hike into Vermont's Green Mountains.

"Oh, Joy, we don't want you in the woods by yourself," my mother said. "You'll die in the woods."

But I didn't give up. I kept pestering my parents. Every day I gave them another reason why I should go to Stowe. When my reasoning didn't work, I tried sulking in my bedroom. Then I moved back to badgering.

It took a while, but my parents finally agreed to at least let me apply. I filled out all the paperwork, and a few weeks later I got a letter back saying I'd earned a partial scholarship. Somehow my father scraped up enough money to pay for the rest of the tuition. I did it. I was in.

When the day arrived for me to leave for Stowe, my mother drove me to the Port Authority terminal in New York City, put me on a bus heading north, and waved goodbye. I remember waving back as the bus pulled away, until my mother disappeared from view.

I was fifteen, and I was on my own for the first time in my life.

I got off the bus in a small New York town called Clinton, in the foothills of the Adirondacks. I put on my bulky backpack and walked slowly toward a group of about seventy other teenagers on the campus of Hamilton College. That was our starting point for the 300-mile hike across the border to northern Vermont.

Very quickly, I realized I was out of place. A lot of the other kids knew each other, and most of them came from really wealthy families. One of the boys was the son of the president of Venezuela. Another one's father was the head of an airline. My dad had a bus company on Long Island.

A familiar feeling gripped me—the feeling of being inferior. But I was used to that feeling, and I knew how to pull myself out of it. I gravitated toward the kids who seemed less snobby than the others and tried to make as many new friends as I could.

Several days into the hike, it was time for us to split up and go solo.

We were all given three matches, a pad of paper, and a pencil. We had no real food, except for some "bark"—this awful, hard, oatmealy thing that tasted like stale granola. That first night in the wilderness on my own was rough. We'd all heard the rumors about a deranged serial killer in the area—the Hatchet Man, they called him. I zipped up my sleeping bag and shut my eyes tight and tried not to think about the Hatchet Man. But every little noise, every rustling leaf, convinced me that I was about to meet my doom.

Somehow I made it through the night. But now there was another challenge—how would I keep myself busy throughout the day? All I had was my pad and pencil, which I guess were supposed to be for me to keep a journal of my inspired thoughts. But I had a better idea.

I carefully tore the pad into fifty-two pieces and made a deck of cards. Whenever I got tired of hiking I'd sit down and play solitaire for a few hours. My handmade deck of cards helped me make it through my three days alone.

For the final leg of the journey, the counselors split us into groups of three, and we followed a path through the Green Mountains and onto the campus of the school itself. My parents drove up to meet me there, mainly because they were worried I might be dead.

"My God," Toots shouted when she saw me, "you look emaciated!"

But I had made it, and I settled in at Stowe. Academically, the school was challenging, and I had to work extra hard on my studies. But I was a good student and stayed a step ahead of the curriculum, and I still had every morning free to do nothing but ski.

Waking up early and skiing the beautiful glades of Mount Mansfield and Spruce Peak, carving new paths through the untouched snow, was a transformative experience for me. One crisp, sunny morning, I skied down a mountain and headed toward a little cliff that I knew was there. Instead of skiing around it like I normally did, I went right at it and flew over the ledge, lifting high into the air, skis over my head, and then coming down and landing softly on the snow.

A perfect flip.

And in that moment, I felt like a magical new person.

Who was this girl flying through the winter air, free and clear of the world? It was me. It was Joy. Only I was different now. I was a little better. A little braver. I felt it then, and I knew what it meant.

*It meant I was discovering a new side of me.*

When I first went into the world of business, I was told that in order to succeed, I had to choose a path for myself and never deviate from it. If I ventured off it even a little bit, I was warned, I would never be able to achieve my goal. I would lose my focus and fail.

That's just not the way I see it, either in business or in life.

Our paths through life will *always* change, whether we want them to or not. No matter how old we are, life offers us constant opportunities to explore new paths and take new adventures, and it serves up constant obstacles that push us into new terrain.

And it is through each of these new paths and adventures that we discover ourselves a little bit more. It is by confronting obstacles that we learn a little more about who we really are, and who we really can be.

That is, as long as we embrace this change and stay ready to go down new paths with as much daring and skill as we can muster.

When I was hurtling down a mountainside at 50 mph, I didn't have the luxury of seeing the whole way down. I just had to get started and see where the mountain took me. And when I saw that I was headed straight for a balsam or a birch or an aspen, I didn't stop. I just shifted my skis, found a new path, and kept right on going as best I could.

In life, and in business, we always need to be ready to shift our skis. If we do, we will never stop discovering ourselves.

At Stowe, it didn't take me long to realize my dream of winning an Olympic gold medal would never come true. Not because I wasn't good enough, but because I was too skinny. I just wasn't heavy enough to generate any real speed down the mountain.

But that was okay. My entire time at Stowe, from the long hike through the mountains to my endless mornings skiing, really and truly changed me. I left home an Olympic long shot, but I came back a more confident, more capable, and more courageous me.

And all because I chose to chase a dream, and I wasn't afraid to shift my skis along the way.

# 7

At Stowe, I packed my schedule with so many classes that I was able to squeeze three years of school into two and graduate a year early. But instead of going straight to college, I headed for a different destination: an animal hospital.

Why? Because I was going to be a veterinarian.

It was something I'd been thinking about since I was little, and my best friend in the world was Duke. When I got older, our family vet diagnosed Duke with cancer. He was twelve and his pain was so bad he had to drag himself around by his front paws.

One afternoon, my father loaded Duke into the car, and we drove him to the veterinarian's office to be put to sleep. It was the worst car ride of my life. I sat in the back with Duke and put my arm around him and tried to let him know how much I loved him. Then I looked at his face and saw that it was wet. Water was coming out of his eyes.

Duke was crying.

I'd never seen a dog cry and I didn't know they could. But I knew without a doubt that's what Duke was doing. He sensed this was our last moment together. And so he cried, and I cried, too, for the whole car ride.

That afternoon, we said goodbye to Duke.

I was devastated. Seeing Duke cry tore my heart to pieces. I'd saved him from the pool, but I just couldn't save him this time.

After Stowe, I thought back to that moment, and I knew what I wanted to devote myself to—I wanted to help other sick dogs like Duke. So I put college aside and looked for a job at an animal hospital.

I typed up a résumé and put on my best white skirt and walked into animal hospitals all over Long Island. I was seventeen and I'd finally graduated from clunky glasses to contact lenses, which helped me feel more confident. At the third hospital I visited, a veterinarian greeted me at the reception desk.

"Can I help you?" he asked.

"I'm looking for a job."

"Then follow me," he said.

The doctor took me to the back and put me right to work as his assistant. Maybe he was testing me to see how I handled pressure. I stayed with him while he performed a couple of routine checkups, and I also helped pet owners fill out paperwork. Nothing too serious, but still, real work. After an hour or so, the doctor handed me a form for a prescription and asked me to fill it out.

"You have to check this box right there," he said.

I went to check the box, but because I'm left-handed, it might have looked to him like I was about to check a different box.

"No, not that box!" the vet said impatiently. "That's the wrong box!"

I was startled, and I shot right back at him, "Excuse me, you don't have to yell at me. I was going to check the right box—see?"

The doctor looked at me for two or three seconds, then smiled.

"You're hired," he said.

His name was Dr. Jeff, and after that we got along great. He was smart and friendly and he taught me a lot about caring for animals.

On top of all his amazing veterinary work, Dr. Jeff created his own brand of pet food. Back then, there weren't any healthy choices as far as pet food went, and Dr. Jeff had an idea to produce a line of natural products for cats and dogs. He knew all the science behind it, and he distributed the food right out of a facility next door to the hospital.

It was my first up-close exposure to how a business worked, and I was mesmerized.

I asked Dr. Jeff if I could help him with the business, and he let me get involved in every facet of it. Before long I was handling the books, arranging deliveries, and helping design new packaging. Dr. Jeff would always tell people I was running the business for him.

But what excited me most was that Dr. Jeff had created something out of nothing. He had willed an idea into existence, and he was helping a lot of animals with it. And that made my own creative instincts start to bubble up again. I felt free and confident and inspired to do something like Dr. Jeff had done.

And then I felt it—a little spark.

The spark of a new idea.

Most of the injured dogs who wound up in the animal hospital were there because they'd been hit by a car. In the suburbs, dogs were especially vulnerable to getting struck by cars, mostly at night, when they were almost impossible to see. In our area, it seemed like a dog got hit by a car every few weeks. Seeing how badly they were injured—if they even survived—was heartbreaking.

So I sat down and thought about the problem. What could I do to make dogs less vulnerable to getting hit by cars? Well, if they were somehow more visible, drivers would have a better chance of seeing them in time.

Okay, but how could I make dogs more visible at night? They needed to be illuminated in some way. Yes, but how? They needed to have some form of lighting on them somehow. Maybe something fluorescent.

But how could you possibly put fluorescent lighting on a dog? Unleashed dogs didn't have anywhere to attach anything.

Except for the one thing most dogs wore in those days.

A flea collar.

This was long before there were any pills or treatments for fleas and ticks, and most dogs wore a simple flea collar that snapped on and off.

But what if . . .

. . . what if that flea collar were fluorescent, too?

I started doing research. I looked into all kinds of fluorescent and reflective materials. I picked the ones I thought could be used to make a flea collar. I made sketches and drawings. The idea seemed to make sense.

When I felt like I knew what I wanted the collar to be, I took my idea to Dr. Jeff. He liked it, and he shared it with some other veterinarians he knew, and they all agreed it was a really good idea, too. I felt like I was really onto something. Now all I had to do was follow through.

And then—nothing.

Nothing happened.

Because I didn't follow through.

Something came up that got me distracted, and then something else, and something after that. Basically all the little things in my teenage life distracted me. I put my idea on the back burner, intending to pursue it as soon as I had the time. A few weeks passed, and the weeks turned into months, and my very good idea stayed just that—an idea.

About a year later, I came across an advertisement for a new product from a major pet supply company.

The ad was for a brand-new, never-before-seen fluorescent flea collar.

I stared at the ad in shock. This was my idea. My flea-collar product. And now it was real, except I didn't have anything to do with it. How could this have happened?

The harsh truth was that I missed my chance. I waited, and the opportunity disappeared. Plain and simple, I blew it.

Having a good idea, I know now, is only the start of a process. Lots of people have good ideas, even great ideas. But if you don't follow through— if you don't pour real energy into the next step, and the step after that, and the step after that—it won't matter how good or great your idea is.

*Because somewhere, someone else has the same idea, and they're probably working really hard to make it real.*

That is the thought that fuels me today. Whenever I have an idea, I assume someone else is working on something very similar, or even identical. I can't be sure anyone is, but I assume *someone* is.

So once I've had the idea—once it's out of my brain and out of my mouth and into the air, floating in the universe—I feel like the clock is ticking. I feel the pressure of time slipping away, and I become impatient to turn my idea into reality.

Once an idea is in the air, we need to act, and act fast. We need to find the urgency that comes with new ideas, and fight distractions, and push forward as quickly as we can. Believe me, we don't have a single minute to waste.

Working with Dr. Jeff at his company made me realize I had a true passion for creating things. So after a year at the animal hospital, I applied to several colleges in order to study business.

The absolute top college on my list was Radcliffe, the sister school to Harvard University in Cambridge, Massachusetts. It was one of the most prestigious colleges in the country, and not easy to get into. But my grades were strong, and I felt like I had a good chance at getting in.

When I got a letter from the college in the mail, I couldn't tear it open fast enough. The first word in the letter was "Congratulations."

I was in!

Being accepted by Radcliffe felt like the start of something wonderful. The minute I said yes to Radcliffe would be the minute my future would begin to fall into place. I couldn't wait.

But I never did say yes to Radcliffe.

It wasn't meant to be.

# 8

One night, there was a knock on the door of my family's home in Dix Hills. My mother opened it, and a woman was standing there.

"Your husband is a real creep, I hope you know," the woman said.

The woman stormed off, and my mother closed the door without a word. She seemed to take it in stride. By then, I already knew my parents were having problems. They were drifting apart. Whenever I visited my friends, their houses were filled with the sounds of people talking and laughing and maybe even arguing. But on any given night in our house, it was dead quiet. No talking, no laughing, and, after a while, no fighting. Just silence.

When I left for Stowe, it was a relief for me. I felt like I was escaping a really gloomy situation. But my absence only made things worse for my parents. They tried different things to get along better, but it was mostly futile. If Rudy took Toots to a museum, she'd say, "Why do I want to go to a museum?" She'd much rather have gone shopping. For a while my parents took a cooking class together, but that didn't connect them, either. They were too different, and they couldn't figure out how to get what they needed from each other.

Still, Toots wasn't prepared for the day my father moved out.

He'd left a few times before, but he'd always come back after a night or two. This time, though, he moved in with a woman who worked as a bus driver in his company. My mother was devastated. This happened when I was working for Dr. Jeff and living at home, so I was there to see just how much it tore Toots apart. Over the next several months, I became her only source of support.

"You can't leave me, Joy," she'd say. "You're all I have."

And I knew I couldn't leave her. It just wasn't an option. She needed me, and I couldn't walk away. Radcliffe was a four-hour drive from Long Island, and if I went there, I'd probably see my parents only a few days each month. I knew that wouldn't be enough for my mother.

So I didn't go to Radcliffe.

Instead, I stayed at home and commuted to Stony Brook University, a state school not far from where I grew up.

A few months after my father moved out, he moved back in. I guess he got tired of his new girlfriend, or maybe she got tired of him. My mother instantly forgave him and took him back in.

But a few months later, he left and moved back in with his girl-friend.

And then, a few months after that, he came home again.

That's how things were with Rudy and Toots for a long time. To-gether, apart, together, apart. It seemed like my parents could never quite leave each other for good. Sometimes, I felt like the Band-Aid that was keeping whatever remained of their marriage intact.

During one breakup, my parents sold their house on Long Island. Then they got back together and rented an apartment in New York City. And then they started pushing apart again.

"You guys have got to stop this," I lectured them one night. "I'm nineteen, and I can't do this anymore. You have got to figure out what it is that you like about each other."

But it was no use. After yet another breakup they gave up their New York City apartment, and my mother and I rented a two-bedroom apartment in Queens, just across the East River from Manhattan.

It was then that something remarkable started to happen.

After Toots and I settled into our apartment, she didn't just sit around the house by herself, waiting for Rudy to come back. Instead of crying and pining, she went out and found a job as an executive assistant at Revlon, the cosmetics company.

The job changed everything for her. For one thing, it allowed her to dress as elegantly as she liked and not seem eccentric for doing it. But it also gave her a confidence I hadn't ever really seen in her before.

After leaving Revlon to work at Bloomingdale's, Toots became the chief assistant to Marjorie Deane, an extremely influential fashion trend-spotter. For decades, Mrs. Deane put out a weekly newsletter, the *Tobe Report*, that was required reading for Macy's and Gimbels and Bloomingdale's and every other major fashion outlet.

My mother and Mrs. Deane spent hundreds of hours together, organizing the report and going to fashion shows while wearing their big, stylish hats.

Sometimes, even in our toughest moments, it's worth taking a step back and comparing who we are to who everyone expects us to be.

What we learn might surprise us.

Both my parents came from families with traditional views about marriage and a lot of other things. Rudy and Toots were both expected to get married, have children, and devote themselves to their family. Rudy would work and earn a salary, while Toots stayed home and raised the kids. That's how families worked. That's what normal families were supposed to be like.

But it didn't work out that way for them.

I'm not saying they were better off without each other. I don't know if they could have ever made their marriage work somehow. But after circling back time and time again, my mother decided to fix what was broken in her life by striking out on her own and becoming a working woman.

At the time, that didn't make her family a "normal" family.

But that didn't matter, because Toots shifted her skis and discovered a new side of herself—and found the person she was meant to be.

Still, just because "normal" didn't work for my parents didn't mean it wouldn't work for me. I still dreamed of having a long, beautiful, happy marriage to a caring, loving husband and a wonderful, functioning family. What happened to my parents wasn't going to happen to me—that was one thing I was sure about.

I was happy to see my mother do something to fix what wasn't working in her life—even if she'd been forced to do it. But I knew my own journey would be different.

# 9

After a year at Stony Brook, I transferred to Pace University, a private school with a great business program in Lower Manhattan. To help pay for my tuition I got a scholarship and took a clerical job in the school's personnel department. I worked twenty hours a week, and when I wasn't working or in class I was studying in my room or at the library. I almost never missed a class.

Even the one time I got sick and couldn't make it to an important sociology lecture, I asked Toots to go for me—and I made her take a tape recorder.

"I can't believe you're making me do this," she said.

I was settling into a routine. I was focused and determined and driven. I had a goal, and my life was neat and regimented.

And then, all of a sudden—BOOM.

It happened in an elevator in a building on the campus of Pace

University. I was on the elevator when a pretty blond girl from one of my classes walked on. Her name was Susette.

"Hey, do you mind if I cheat off you on our quiz today?" she asked. "I didn't study at all."

I wasn't sure how to answer, but before I even had the chance to open my mouth, Susette said, "You know what, let's just blow it off."

Blow off the test? On purpose? That wasn't who I was. I mean, I would *never* do something like that. I was about to shake my head and politely decline.

But, for some reason, I didn't.

Instead, I said, "Okay."

And so Susette and I got off the elevator, skipped the test, and went to the school pub instead.

I didn't know why I had said okay to Susette. It just happened. It was like a little voice in my head chirped, *Go ahead, do it!* As if some fateful cosmic force was guiding me instead of my own logic and sense. I should have felt bad about skipping the test, but I didn't feel the least bit guilty. It was like missing the quiz was somehow meant to happen.

I hadn't been to the university pub before, and when Susette and I walked in, I was startled. The pub was dark and loud and alive. People were everywhere, talking and drinking and laughing and dancing, and the atmosphere was electric. I'd never experienced so much energy and excitement in one place before.

The pub was the very opposite of my quiet, studious life.

Susette led me to the bumper pool table, where her brothers Tony (her dark-haired twin) and Alan were playing a game.

Tony, I could tell right away, was the center of attention.

He was very handsome and had girls hanging all over him. He was funny and outgoing and charismatic and so sure of himself—more confident than anyone I'd ever known. He seemed to exert a kind of magnetic pull that made you want to be around him.

Being with Susette and Tony in the pub was a remarkable experience. Songs were blasting out of the jukebox, everyone was having fun, and it was all so exciting and vital and crazy. Then we got hungry and someone said, "Let's go to Chinatown for dinner!" Just like that, we all went to Hop Kee's, and the food was the most delicious I'd ever eaten. Or maybe it just seemed that way, because everything that day felt so heightened and intense.

And then, all of a sudden, I realized something.

I realized that I *loved* it.

I loved what was happening around me. I loved being a part of it all. The music, the food, the people, the laughter, everything. I'd been the girl who never went to parties, never had a boyfriend, never hung out in bars, never did anything crazy—but that day I finally saw everything I'd been missing.

And I knew it was *exactly* what I needed in my life.

I'm still not entirely sure what made me skip the quiz that day. Susette was a beautiful, vivacious person with a special energy, so maybe that's why I followed her to the pub. What I do know for sure is that, because I did, my life is what it is today.

That moment shaped what would become one of the driving forces of my life—the belief that everything happens for a reason.

Sometimes we need to allow ourselves to be guided out of our comfort zones. We need to listen to our most powerful instincts and let them lead us where they will. I absolutely felt like some force was guiding me to go with Susette to the pub that day. I didn't understand it, but the feeling was so strong that I gave into it. Had Susette showed up just a minute later, my life would be so completely different. But she showed up just when she did, right before the elevator closed, and my life changed forever.

Everything happens for a reason.

Believing this is true will lead us to change the way we perceive certain events in our lives—especially events that might otherwise seem really bad or troubling. It will affect how we react to these events, which in turn will shape the course of our lives.

If we can believe that everything happens for a reason—and then stay open to whatever that reason may be—we'll be able to handle challenges and adversity with more confidence and more success.

So let's stay open to our strongest instincts and allow them to guide us. Let's not be afraid to try something totally out of character if we feel life pulling us that way. We might become someone different, but different doesn't mean bad. Different just means we had the courage to explore who we're really supposed to be.

After that day, I still went to all my classes, and I never stopped being a good student. But instead of going straight home after my classes and my job, I began stopping by the pub a few times a week.

One day, I met Susette and Tony there, and they were arguing about something.

"No, I'm not gonna do it," Susette said.

"Come on, you have to do it," Tony insisted.

Susette was balking at one of Tony's schemes. He had a final exam and he hadn't studied for it, and his plan was to tell the professor he'd been in a car accident and hurt his leg and couldn't take the test. He needed Susette to help him sell the story.

Finally, she agreed, and we wrapped Tony's leg in a big bandage and he limped into the professor's office, with Susette pretending to hold him up. I stayed behind at the pub.

Not much later, Tony and Susette came back.

"He bought it!" Tony announced, a big, bright grin on his face.

I laughed and wondered, *Who does this kind of thing?*

The answer made me feel really happy.

*My friends, that's who.*

# 10

Tony and Susette were a year ahead of me at Pace, and they graduated at the end of my junior year. That summer, my friend Allison threw a party in her family's Long Island house, and she invited all of us. By then, I wasn't skinny Joy anymore. I was nineteen and athletic. For the party I wore tight white jeans and a striped peach tube top that showed off my deep summer tan. I drove my father's big white Cadillac to Allison's house and found everyone playing volleyball out back.

When Tony turned around and saw me, his jaw dropped.

I guess he'd never seen me all dressed up like that.

At the party, both Tony and Alan stayed pretty close to me. It was Tony on one side and Alan on the other. This was something brand-new for me. I wasn't the girl whose attention guys vied for. But here it was, happening anyway.

Halfway through the party, Tony pointed at my dad's Cadillac.

"You know, the air pressure on your right rear tire is low," he said. "You shouldn't drive back home with your tire like that."

"Really?" I said. "Thanks for letting me know."

"We can go and fill it up now if you want," Tony said.

Tony had worked part-time in a garage that was only a short drive away. We got into the Cadillac and I drove us there. On the way, Tony said something that completely knocked me off balance.

"So, you going out with anyone?" he asked.

"Uh, no," I said.

"Me neither," Tony said.

And right then is when I drove the Cadillac over a curb.

You see, Tony was a hotshot. He was handsome and charming and magnetic, and I really liked being around him. He had all kinds of girls circling him, yet here he was, asking me if *I* had a boyfriend. I couldn't believe it was happening.

The next day, Tony called and asked me out on a date.

I said yes.

On one of our first dates, Tony and I went to a popular disco in New York City. We danced and drank beer and listened to a band play, and Tony told jokes and funny stories that made me laugh until I cried. Being out with Tony was so *freeing*. It felt like I was on a big adventure where anything could happen. That night at the club, Tony even jumped onstage and sang with the band. He had a great voice, and he was a natural entertainer. I don't remember what song he sang, but I do remember how I felt as I watched him pour his heart into it.

I felt happier than I ever had before.

Tony was my first serious boyfriend, and he swept me away. Everything we did together was filled with fun and laughter. This was around the time that John Travolta and *Saturday Night Fever* were all the rage, and Tony and I went to all the exciting new discos, and we did the Hustle and the Funky Chicken and all those other dances.

Other times, we'd drive out to the beach and just walk along the water. And once or twice a week, Tony would swing by the apartment I shared with my mother in Queens and make us both laugh. Toots liked Tony instantly; in fact, he was the one who nicknamed her Toots. She liked the same things about him I did—his energy, his humor, his liveliness. He'd pop through the door and say, "Let's go get Pastrami King!" and off we'd go, on another adventure.

But it wasn't just Tony who swept me away. It was his family, too.

A few months after we started dating, I went to a party at the home of Tony's parents, in the town of Elmont on Long Island. His two brothers and two sisters were there, as well as dozens of other relatives and friends. I went to Susette's bedroom, and she pulled out the trundle bed and five or six of us girls sat there and talked and laughed. Tony's mother was in the kitchen cooking an enormous meal, and delicious smells wafted through the house. Tony's father was telling a funny story to a group of people in the living room. A bit later, Tony himself got up in front of everyone and belted out a song.

This was the most spirited, charming, magical family I'd ever seen.

The more I learned about them, the more I loved them. Tony's father, Joe, was part French, part German, part Irish, and part something else. He was born into a wealthy southern family from New Orleans, and his parents ran a large and prosperous savings-and-loan business. Joe had been expected to enter the family business and become a banker, just like his brother and his father and his father's father before them. His path in life had been carved out for him since birth.

But Joe had other ideas.

When World War II broke out, he enlisted in the navy, and at the age of twenty-eight he captained a boat that stormed Utah Beach during the 1944 Allied landings in Normandy, France. Though he never talked about it in later years, he was a true war hero.

When Joe got back from the war, he went against his parents' wishes and followed his dream of being a singer. He moved to New York City and began auditioning for movies and musicals. One day, a Manhattan talent agent was supposed to watch him sing at an audition, but he couldn't make it and sent his assistant instead. The assistant, a twenty-year-old from a Czechoslovakian family named Martha, was dazzled by Joe's singing—and Joe was dazzled by her beauty. But she was already friendly with another singer at the talent agency.

Joe didn't let that stop him, and eventually he won Martha's heart.

The other singer's name was Dean Martin.

Joe and Martha got married and had five children. Tony, their fourth child (by just two minutes—his twin sister, Susette, narrowly beat him out), grew up idolizing his father. If Joe went to the grocery store, Tony went with him. If Joe stood up and sang a song, Tony sang one, too. I understood why Tony was so captivated by his father, because I was captivated by him, too. Joe was someone who had turned away from his preordained future—and guaranteed riches—and carved out a brave new path for himself. And when his singing career didn't take off and he and Martha had to raise five children with barely enough money to survive, he stuck with his passion and started teaching speech and drama at Pace University. He became the chair of the Speech and Drama department, and he even had the campus theater named after him.

And Martha? Her parents were dirt-poor immigrants who didn't speak a word of English when they came to America. Some of Joe's relatives felt she wasn't good enough or smart enough for him. But Martha found the man of her dreams, had five children, scraped up every penny to make ends meet, went to school, earned a master's degree in economics, and became a respected professor at Pace University, teaching on the same faculty as her husband.

What stories! What lives! Joe and Martha were enormously inspiring to me, because they had struck out on their own and carved their own paths, fighting and pushing and dreaming and believing in each other every step of the way.

Just because something has never been done doesn't mean it can't be done. The essence of a creative life is carving your own path.

My mother, Toots, carved her own path after Rudy left, and she found happiness and fulfillment. And Tony's father, Joe, was expected to follow in the family tradition and become a banker. His life was totally laid out for him. But both he and Martha carved their own paths. It was hard, but together they built a full and happy and joyful life.

As an inventor, I've always believed that just because something doesn't exist doesn't mean it *can't* exist. The same is true of anything we choose to do in life. There is no set path for us—we are free to break from tradition and take new adventures.

And if we stumble or feel lost or a little out to sea along the way, we should look at that as proof that we're alive and growing and fighting and daring to invent lives of our own.

# 11

Tony came into my life at exactly the right time. Just when my parents' marriage was unraveling, Tony showed up and lifted me out of the darkness. He replaced the quiet and heaviness of my family's household with songs and jokes and laughter. Tony was the hero who swooped in and saved me from myself.

That first summer we started dating, I fell in love with him.

He proposed to me at Nicola Paone, one of my father's favorite restaurants in Manhattan. I said yes. Tony later told me that, two weeks before we were set to get married, one of his uncles, a cruise-ship director with show-business connections, pulled him aside and tried to convince him not to go through with the wedding.

"You've got talent," his uncle told him. "I will make you a big star. You'll have all the women and the money you could want."

"No, thanks," Tony said. "I love this girl, and I'm going to marry her."
And that's just what he did.

Our wedding was at the Fox Hollow Country Club in Muttontown, Long Island. I arranged everything and got a great deal on the country club because they were closing it and turning it into condos. It was a little tattered around the edges, but it was still very grand and lovely.

My mother wore a custom-made dress, and I wore a sample gown I bought at Kleinfeld's in Brooklyn for $300. It was the first wedding dress I had tried on. Susette was one of my bridesmaids, and so was Kim, the girl Tony's brother Alan was dating when we all first met. My parents, who were separated, sat at different tables and managed not to get into a fight. My mother insisted Rudy couldn't bring any of his girlfriends to the wedding, and, thankfully, he didn't.

At the reception, Tony's father got up and serenaded us with our wedding song, "Les Bicyclettes de Belsize," a beautiful melody made famous by Engelbert Humperdinck.

Then Tony followed his father to the microphone.

Tony wanted to be an entertainer, just like Joe did. When Tony was growing up, there were lots of parties at his home, and Joe's guests included a number of famous artists who passed through the drama department at Pace. Tony told me that one night, Gene Kelly taught him a few dance steps in the basement. Tony believed that entertaining was his destiny, and he dreamed of becoming the next Tom Jones.

I believed Tony could make his dream come true. I believed in him. At our wedding, when he took the microphone from his father, he sang with so much passion and joy, and as I watched him I couldn't stop smiling.

He was doing what he loved, and he was so *alive*. He was shining! That moment was one of the most magical moments of my life.

I still remember the song Tony sang.

It was "My Way."

By then I'd graduated from Pace University, and I was working as a customer service representative for Eastern Air Lines. It wasn't anything I thought I'd be doing, but it was a really good job, and we needed the money, because Tony was just getting started in his singing career.

At Eastern, I went from being a ticket agent to managing the ticket agents to running the customer service desk at the airport. I was the one who had to tell people their flights had been canceled. One night, a customer came up to the desk and asked me a question. I looked up and saw that it was Jackie Onassis.

"Can you tell me how to get to the Ionosphere Club?" she said in her distinctive breathy voice.

"I'll take you there!" I practically yelled, and I slammed the cash drawer shut so fast I caught my hand in it and nearly crushed it. I kept my mangled limb behind my back as I giddily walked Jackie O to the club.

My best friend at Eastern was a woman named Jan, who I met in the ladies' room. Back then, we both had really old cars. I had a yellow Chevy Impala with practically no brakes, and I had to start tapping on the brake pad a hundred feet before an intersection in order to stop in time. Meanwhile, Jan's beat-up old Mustang had a front door that didn't open, so she had to roll down the window and crawl out of the car.

One cold winter night, we both ran straight from our cars to the restroom, and we both reached for the automatic hand dryer at the same time. Our fingers were frozen and we wanted to warm them up.

"I'm sorry, I don't have any heat in my car," I explained.

"Neither do I!" Jan laughed.

We became fast friends after that.

The best part of working at Eastern, though, was that it allowed Tony and me to fly for free. One of the reasons I took the job was because we'd get to fly to Las Vegas to see Tony's idol Tom Jones sing. After our wedding, we also got to fly to Hawaii for our honeymoon. The second leg of the honeymoon would be to Las Vegas, where we'd see a couple of shows and try some nice restaurants and maybe hit a casino or two.

Our first night in Las Vegas, Tony went to the casino without me because I was tired. I thought he'd be there for a couple of hours, but he didn't make it back to the room until 6:00 a.m.

"I love this!" he said as he burst through the door. "This place is the best!"

Tony was caught up in the exciting Vegas atmosphere. The lights, the action, the gambling. Actually, he was more than just caught up in it. He was absolutely intoxicated by it.

I saved up money from my job at Eastern, and Tony and I bought a small, ranch-style three-bedroom, one-bathroom home in East Meadow, Long Island. To help make ends meet while he was going out on auditions and singing in nightclubs, Tony took a job as a salesman for Campbell's Soup. I was working the graveyard shift at the airport.

We didn't get to see each other a lot during that time. I even had to work the night before Christmas. I came home early that morning and walked through the front door crying, because I hated that my job had ruined Christmas Eve with my husband. Tony was sleeping in our bedroom, so I slumped down on the sofa, exhausted. It didn't feel like much of a holiday at all.

That's when I saw it.

It was in the dining room. A fake Christmas tree. Tony had set it up while I was gone, and he'd sprayed it with artificial snow, though most of the snow wound up on the sliding glass door and not the tree itself. It was kind of scrawny and a little wobbly, and it was leaning to one side.

But to me, it was the most beautiful Christmas tree I'd ever seen.

Being married to Tony was wonderful, and we were so happy together—just the two of us against the world. But then, about a year into our marriage, something unexpected happened.

One morning, there was a knock on the door. Tony answered it.

Standing there, holding a suitcase, was my father, Rudy.

"Hello, champ," my father said.

Rudy always called Tony champ. Tony hated that.

"Listen," my father said, "I broke up with Barbara and I'm gonna be here for three weeks, then I'll get out of your hair."

Then Rudy brushed past Tony and went down to the basement.

Tony stood there in shock. You see, he and my father didn't get along. They grated on each other. My father had never approved of Tony as a husband, and Tony thought my father was always working some angle. And now, Rudy was invading Tony's home. We'd just refinished the basement because Tony wanted to practice his singing down there, and he had built himself a bar and brought in a big sectional sofa. It was his cherished private space.

Then Rudy showed up and took it away.

It didn't help that my father had a real knack for getting under people's skin. For instance, he constantly jiggled loose change in his pocket. It was annoying to me, but it drove Tony *crazy*. When Tony lost his job at Campbell's Soup, things between them only got worse.

"Shouldn't you be out looking for a job, champ?" I'd hear my father ask him.

The three weeks turned into three months, and the three months turned into six months.

My father wound up staying with us for a year and a half.

Many times, Tony begged me to tell Rudy to leave.

"Joy, it's time," he'd say. "He's not going to go unless you push him out the door."

"Where's he going to go?" I'd say. "He's my father, I can't just kick him out."

I felt really bad for Tony, but I didn't know what to do. There was no way I could tell my father to leave. He was my family. Rudy could also sense when we got especially tired of him, and that's when he'd come home with a case of wine for us, or something like that, and everything would be okay for a while. Rudy also knew enough to stay down in the basement when my mother came to visit so she wouldn't run into him.

"Your father better not be there when I come," my mother would say.

It wasn't the best situation for anyone, but it was what it was. I knew full well that with my family, at least, there was no such thing as normal. We all just had to find a way to make it through the craziness.

And that's when I got pregnant.

# 12

I was twenty-six when I went into labor. Tony helped me into the car and drove us onto the Long Island Expressway, headed for North Shore University Hospital. Traffic was really bad on the LIE, and it was going to take us forever to drive just a few miles.

But Tony didn't like to wait. He didn't like to wait for anything—not on lines, not in restaurants, and certainly not on the LIE. So he pulled the car onto the grass partition alongside the slow lane and sped past all the traffic at high speed. Remarkably, we didn't get pulled over, and we made it to the hospital in record time.

Tony also hated hospitals. He'd get queasy, then grouchy, whenever he was around IVs or blood bags or anything medical. This was my first labor, and like a lot of first labors it was long and difficult, and progressively harder with each passing hour. Tony was a wreck the whole time. He was queasy and then grouchy nonstop.

"Honey, can you get me some ice chips?" I asked him at one point.

"Do you really need ice chips?" he said. "Do you really?"

Then it was time. Tony came with me to the delivery room. I knew he didn't want to be there. I knew he had to physically fight himself to not run out of the room. But to his credit, he stayed. One of the nurses told him to get down by my side and hold my hand and help me push. Tony shook his head and stepped backward until his feet were flush against a wall. He stayed there, clinging to the safety of the wall, for the whole delivery, while the nurse knelt beside me and held my hand.

Finally, our child arrived. We named her Christie.

Tony and I had talked about having children, and we decided we wanted to have them early on. Tony came from a big, boisterous family, and he told me he wanted that for himself, and I wanted it, too. I wanted five children, just like Tony's parents had. I wanted to have them when I was young, and I wanted to have them all quickly, so they'd be around the same age and get along better.

After Tony lost his job, he spent most of his nights singing in local clubs. I was supportive, because I knew how much singing meant to him. I even helped pay for singing lessons. But once I got pregnant, things changed. We had a child on the way, and Tony knew he had to find a way to support his family. So he took another sales job, with Wise Foods.

Part of Tony's new job was entertaining clients. And one thing Tony could do really well was entertain. He'd take clients out on long dinners, treat them to baseball games, invite them to Broadway shows, or just go out drinking with them. At work, he came to be known as the King of Entertainment. Most nights, I had no idea where he was or when he'd get home, and usually he wouldn't make it back until 2:00 a.m. or later. I told him that when the baby came, he would need to keep shorter hours.

"That's the job," Tony said.

The thought of being a mother was already pretty scary, and not having Tony around made me even more anxious.

But the instant the nurse handed my daughter Christie to me, all those feelings went away. In their place, I felt a new depth of love that was just astounding. It was breathtaking. I felt it wash over me in big waves, and it never stopped. I held on to Christie and I looked at her perfect little face with awe. Her eyes were shut tight, and her tiny pink fingers were clenched, except for one pinkie, which was straight. I kissed her gently on the cheek, and I realized I was crying.

And then Tony held Christie, and I could tell he was overwhelmed, too. I could see the love he had for her on his big smiling face, and when he gently rocked her and kissed her I felt something like pure bliss.

We were a family now.

A few hours after Christie was born, Tony went home while I stayed in the hospital to nurse her overnight. The next day would be a very big day—the day Tony came back to the hospital to bring his wife and new daughter home. Our first full day together as a family.

That morning, a nurse helped me wrap Christie in a pretty pink blanket, and she held her while I got myself dressed and ready. Then I sat on the bed with Christie in my arms and waited for Tony to arrive. I watched other husbands walk by my room, then walk by again with their wives and new babies in tow. I couldn't wait for Tony to come get us.

But then 11:00 a.m., the time Tony was supposed to show up, came and went. I waited patiently. Ten minutes passed, then thirty minutes, then an hour. Still no Tony.

I kissed Christie and told her her father would be there soon.

But Tony never came.

# 13

After more than an hour of waiting, I finally called Vickie, our neighbor across the street in East Meadow.

"Vickie, is Tony's car in the driveway?" I asked.

Vickie took a second to look out the window.

"Yeah, it's there."

"Can you do me a favor and see if Tony's home?"

Vickie went over and knocked on the front door. Nothing happened. She knocked again and again, but still, nothing.

"No one's answering," she told me.

Then I called Ronny Lee. He was a friend who was helping Tony do some work on our bathroom.

"Ronny Lee, you have the keys to the house. Can you go inside and see if Tony's there? He might be sleeping."

Ronny Lee found Tony in our bedroom, passed out on top of the bed.

He tried to rouse him, but it was clear Tony was in no shape to come to the hospital on his own. So Ronny Lee got him on his feet, put him in the back of our station wagon, and drove him to North Shore Hospital. When they got there, he tried to pull Tony out of the car, but it was no use. Tony was staying put.

A nurse wheeled me down to the lobby, and Ronny Lee came in and helped me bundle Christie into her car seat. I could see from the look on Ronny Lee's face that he was crushed for me. This should have been a beautiful, happy moment, one that Tony and I would remember forever. Instead it was the lowest point of our marriage so far. I tried not to let Ronny Lee see how distraught I was.

Back at home, Tony went straight to the couch and sprawled out. My mother was on her way, and Ronny Lee offered to stick around until she got there. I felt like I might break down and cry, but I didn't. Instead, I got busy and pretended like everything was fine.

When Tony finally woke up hours later, he explained he'd been celebrating Christie's birth with Susette and Alan, and things got out of hand. He said he hadn't eaten anything because he was queasy from the hospital, and he drank too many Rusty Nails on an empty stomach. For the next few days Tony was apologetic and helpful and on his best behavior. I knew he was feeling a lot of pressure now that Christie was here, and so was I. We just had to find a way to deal with it together.

Six months later, I was pregnant again.

Our second child, Bobby, arrived six weeks early. He weighed six pounds, and he was born with his feet curled up instead of straight out. Just a week after his birth, the doctors had to put his legs in cylinder casts. Every two weeks I had to soak them off and put new ones on. I'd been a sickly infant myself, but I had no idea what that actually entailed. Seeing our tiny baby in bulky leg casts was emotionally devastating.

One night when Bobby was six weeks old, I couldn't get him to stop crying. I tried everything, but nothing worked. And it wasn't a normal cry, either; I could tell something was wrong. Tony, naturally, was out with clients. It was 2:00 a.m. and I hated to do it, but I called Tony's brother Alan, who lived nearby with his wife, Kim. I asked Kim if she could babysit Christie while I took Bobby to the emergency room. She came right over.

My father drove us to the hospital, where our pediatrician, Dr. Sussman, examined Bobby. Bobby was severely dehydrated—so dehydrated that the nurse couldn't even put an IV in his arm. Instead, she tried to connect one to a spot on his forehead, but she missed, and his forehead blew up like a golf ball. I felt a sick, terrible, ominous feeling. I felt like something horrible was unfolding right in front of me. I felt like I wanted to cry out to the heavens for help.

A little while later, Tony showed up at the hospital. Dr. Sussman told us he was worried Bobby might have hepatitis, and said he was ordering a spinal tap. When I heard the words spinal tap, I flipped out.

"No!" I screamed. "No, no, no!"

I looked at Bobby, and his skin was gray. This could not be real. This could not be my life. This had to be a really terrible dream.

But then, a miracle happened.

By sheer coincidence, a world-renowned pediatrician named Dr. Seo happened to be coming out of surgery at North Shore at 3:00 a.m., which was when we were there with Bobby. It was an unbelievable stroke of good luck. Dr. Sussman stopped Dr. Seo in the hallway and asked him to take a look at Bobby.

Dr. Seo immediately knew what was wrong. Bobby had pyloric stenosis, an extremely rare condition that caused his stomach muscles to close up and prevented any food or liquid from getting into his body. Bobby was throwing up anything we gave him, and he was getting weaker and weaker by the minute. His little body was starving.

Dr. Seo said we had to operate on him right away.

Only later did I learn that Bobby was just hours away from dying.

Dr. Seo couldn't perform the operation himself because he'd just come out of surgery. So he called one of his colleagues, who rushed to the hospital. Tony and I watched together as the doctors stretched Bobby out on a regular-size stainless-steel operating table, his tiny legs still in casts. The sight of him on that cold table made me want to cry, but I was too scared to cry. The surgical team wheeled Bobby into the operating room, and Tony and I sat in the waiting room for the next five hours.

Finally, one of the doctors came out and told us we could see our son.

I wasn't prepared for what I saw. Bobby had tubes coming out of everywhere. It didn't seem possible that a creature so small could have so many tubes sticking out of his body. I went to him and lowered my face next to his and heard him let out a tiny cry—just a whimper, really, like a wounded bird. It was the most heartbreaking sound I'd ever heard, and I felt so helpless and lost. There was nothing I could do to make Bobby's tiny little crying stop.

I stayed in the hospital for the next three days, holding Bobby's hand and sleeping curled up on a two-seat sofa in his room. After a couple of days, the doctors let me go back to nursing him. Finally, I got to bring Bobby home. He was only seven weeks old, and he'd already been through hell. We all had.

Despite the ordeal of Bobby's illness, Tony and I still wanted a big, noisy family. Less than two years after Bobby was born, our daughter Jackie arrived.

Both Christie and Bobby had been jaundiced, and Jackie was, too, only her situation was more serious. Soon after her birth, she had to be moved to the intensive care unit. The doctors had to run constant tests on her and keep track of her temperature, and she had to be supervised around the clock until her blood-cell count could be controlled. That meant she had to stay in the hospital for several days.

I wanted to stay with her, but the doctors said I couldn't. Instead, I had to leave my precious newborn, Jackie, in the hospital all by herself. That was one of the hardest things I've ever had to do in my life. I insisted that I wanted to nurse her, and the doctors let me do it, so six times a day I drove forty-five minutes each way to the hospital so I could be with Jackie.

That was a really trying time. I'd leave Bobby and Christie with my mother or Kim or my grandmother Mimi, who lived in Brooklyn and would come out and stay with us. But every time I left my children to go to the hospital, they would cry. And that would make *me* cry. And every time I had to say goodbye to Jackie at the hospital, I would cry some more.

This went on for several days. I wasn't working at Eastern Air Lines anymore, after they gave me the choice of staying on the graveyard shift or quitting. Tony was still working at Wise, and he always seemed to have a sales call to go on or a client to check in with or an event that kept him out late, which meant that most nights I was home alone with the three children. None of them were great sleepers, so some nights I barely slept at all. I was never not exhausted.

But what could I do besides keep going?

# 14

I was having more and more trouble sleeping. I was eating less and less. As the weeks passed, I felt ever more run-down. I felt like I'd been either pregnant or nursing nonstop for the last four years, which was basically true. It was all by my own choosing, I knew that. No one told us to have three kids in four years. But neither Tony nor I were ready for how grueling—mentally, emotionally, and physically—having three children that quickly would be.

But still, I believed that if I could just sleep for more than a couple of hours for one night—just one night—I would be okay.

One evening, when Tony was out with a client, I finally got the children to sleep and staggered into bed. I was completely drained of energy. Tired down to my bones. I fell into an unusually deep sleep.

But then I was jolted awake by a wave of nausea and a gripping pain in my stomach. I pulled myself out of bed and staggered to the bathroom and sat down on the cold floor. The pain in my stomach got worse, and I doubled over and curled up into a ball and threw up. I didn't know what was happening to me.

Suddenly, I felt a terrible, overwhelming sensation.

I felt like the bathroom walls were collapsing on top of me. Like everything in the bathroom—tub, sink, mirror—was being sucked right into my body. The weight and the pressure I felt were crushing. I curled up even tighter and held my head in my hands, trying to stop my brain from exploding. And still everything kept collapsing on me, pushing me down, pinning me to the floor. I sank deeper into myself and lay my head on the tile, and then I couldn't move at all. I felt paralyzed. Something was terribly wrong, and I didn't know what. I was scared to death.

Somehow, I had to get help. If I didn't, I was afraid I would die. There was a wall phone in the kitchen, which was about twenty feet away. I willed my arms to move and dragged myself to the kitchen an inch at a time, my head never rising off the floor. It took me a long time to get to the kitchen, and even longer to get the phone off its cradle, high up on the wall. But I finally got it in my hands, and I called my mother.

"Mom, something is happening to me. Something bad."

"Where's Tony?" she asked.

I said I didn't know.

"Just lie down and call me back in a while if you don't feel better."

Now I was panicking. I knew if one of the children woke up, I wouldn't be able to get to them. I felt completely powerless. Out of desperation I called my sister-in-law, Kim, and asked her to come over. She showed up in fifteen minutes and watched out for the kids while I dragged myself to the sofa, barely able to lift my head.

It was the longest night of my life.

The sun was coming up when Tony finally came home. Kim was furious with him.

"Joy is sick," she told him.

"With what?"

"We don't know."

Tony came over to see me, but just for a few minutes. Then he snuck off to the bedroom and fell asleep.

It was right then—right at that moment—that I realized exactly how much trouble I was in.

My biggest fear was that I might have some devastating virus that would incapacitate me for weeks or even months. And if I did, I understood that I wouldn't be able to count on Tony to take care of me or the children. That just wasn't going to happen.

I'd never, ever felt as vulnerable as I did in that moment.

"Kim . . ." I said.

"Don't say it," she said, cutting me off. "I get it. This isn't a one-night thing. This is going to take a long time."

She was right. It took a long time.

# 15

There was no diagnosis, not at first, anyway. The best my doctor could come up with was exhaustion. My body was critically run-down. He told me that if I'd been older or had high blood pressure, I would have had a heart attack.

"You cannot survive on no sleep," he said. "You need to sleep more."

An internist tested my blood and concluded that there was nothing wrong with me that a few days' rest couldn't cure.

"You're stressed out," he said. "Take a vacation."

When I told people what had happened, I heard the phrase "nervous breakdown" a lot, which back then had a negative stigma attached to it. It suggested the problem was all in my head. But I knew it wasn't. What I went through was *physical*. My brain didn't shut down, my body did.

Still, I didn't believe my problem was simple exhaustion or stress, or a panic attack or anxiety attack or anything like that. What I went through was an intense and violent and systemic upheaval. My whole world came crashing down on me. I felt like I'd plunged to the bottom of a deep, deep well, and I honestly didn't know if I could ever claw my way back to the surface.

My symptoms continued for weeks. Waves of nausea, bouts of panic. Each day I turned everything over in my head, trying to figure out what was happening.

As for Tony, he was genuinely afraid I might die. He knew I was determined to put a name to what was wrong with me, and in his own way he tried to help. One afternoon, he watched an episode of *Oprah* that was devoted to a medical phenomenon afflicting new mothers. Tony ran straight to Toots, who was helping us with the children.

"I know what's wrong with Joy," he announced. "She has postpartum depression."

To Tony, and to many other people, that was the diagnosis that made the most sense. PPD is a clinical depression that can leave you feeling deep sadness, anxiety, and irritability. It can make you feel like you have no energy. Much of that seemed to fit, but I truly didn't believe that I was depressed. There was no dark cloud hanging over me, and I rarely cried. It was just that my body fell apart.

I felt like I couldn't properly function as a mother anymore, or even as a person.

For four years it never dawned on me that I was mistreating my body. I never made the connection between the health of my body and the health of my mind. I was an athlete, a skier, a go-getter. I did flips off mountain slopes. I ran on instinct and natural energy. What was the big deal about having three children and losing some sleep? I could handle it. I was young. I was invincible.

What I didn't realize was that having three children in four years was the biggest challenge I'd ever undertaken in my life. By far. I never considered that I had to take care of myself as well as take care of my children. I didn't eat a healthy diet or take vitamins. I didn't worry about how little I slept. I just kept going. I was like a zombie, absently moving from task to task without even thinking about it.

I was trying to do it all, and I was trying to be perfect.

And that was a mistake.

Sometimes in life, we feel like we have to be box-checkers. We devise a master plan, and we draw up a list, and we don't stop until we check off every box on that list. We strive for perfection.

But none of us is perfect, and none of us needs to be. Perfection is exhausting, and it shouldn't be our goal, anyway. I tried to do it all, and I learned the hard way that I couldn't. I literally broke down trying.

It's okay not to check every box or cross off every to-do. In life, we will all miss an important event or forget someone's birthday, and we'll all feel bad about it. And someone will tell us, "Well, you should have done this or that," and that will make us feel even worse.

But it's okay to sometimes come up short, and it's okay to feel bad about it. It doesn't matter what anyone else thinks about our accomplishments—all that matters is that we do what we need to do to be authentically happy. Putting pressure on ourselves to be perfect just makes an already difficult journey that much harder.

When I think about that tired young mother lying on the cold bathroom tile, I feel so bad for her. I wish I could just hug her and help her feel better about herself.

I wish I could tell her what I know now—that you can't do it all, and you don't *need* to do it all, so please, don't even try.

After my breakdown, I stayed at home for almost six months, trying to get my strength back. I went to see several different doctors until I found one I really liked. He told me my hormone and thyroid levels had been way off, and he gave me B$_{12}$ shots and put me on a solid regimen of vitamins. Slowly, I began to nurse my body back to health.

In the end, I never really got a definitive diagnosis that captured what I'd gone through and how I felt.

But I also realized that wasn't the question that mattered.

The only question that really mattered was, *What do I need to change in my life to make sure I'm never this vulnerable again?*

# 16

A few months after my breakdown, Tony came up to me one afternoon and said he needed me to come with him to a bar to see one of the people he placed bets with.

"You stay in the car, and if I don't come back out in five minutes, leave without me," he said.

"What?" I said. "What are you talking about?"

I knew Tony was betting on sports. I knew that was how he was dealing with the stress. The time I spent seeing doctors and building myself back up cut into the time I'd normally devote to handing all the family obligations—christenings, birthday parties, play dates. More responsibility fell on Tony, and I could tell he didn't like it. When he was home he'd sit on the sofa and watch football games and place bets. That was how he tried to escape the pressure.

But taking me with him to see someone he placed bets with? That was a new level of craziness. I quickly figured out that Tony truly believed there was a chance he wouldn't make it out of the bar alive. Having me there, he reasoned, might make it harder for someone to do something bad to him.

Tony did make it back to the car in one piece.

But that incident was the last straw for me.

Tony moved out of our bedroom and down to the basement. That gave him more freedom to come and go as he pleased. Sometimes we'd have an argument and he'd go sleep in the car. But mostly we just avoided each other. It was easier that way.

But it wasn't the way it should be.

The further apart we drifted, the more our home fell into the terrible emptiness I'd known in my childhood. Two people floating through their lives, together but not really together. And I knew that I didn't want that.

The truth is, Tony wasn't ready for the life we chose for ourselves, and I guess I wasn't, either. We were too young to really understand what having a big family entailed. When the pressure started to build, we both had bad reactions to it. Tony retreated further into nightlife and sports. I wound up on the bathroom floor.

The reality of being parents was very different from anything we'd envisioned. It was much, much harder than we had expected. We both tried to be the people we needed each other to be.

But in the end, we both just broke.

When I was little, I believed in Prince Charming. I thought that was how love worked. After all, my Barbie had a Prince Charming—handsome, dependable Ken. Early on, I believed my father was my mother's Prince Charming. Okay, so that didn't work out, but who could fault me for believing my own Prince Charming would, one day, arrive?

And then he did, and things went wrong anyway.

The night my body stopped working in the bathroom of my house was the first crack in my innocent view of romance and love. And the day Tony took me with him to that bar was the day I understood Prince Charming was never going to come and rescue me.

I'm not saying there aren't any Prince Charmings out there. I am sure there are. But I believe the responsibility for making our lives work better is ours and ours alone. Creating the lives we want for ourselves, and fixing what might be broken in them, is something we need to do on our own.

After my breakdown, I knew I could never allow myself to feel as vulnerable and helpless as I did during that time. I remember talking to myself and saying just that, over and over again.

*Joy, you better get ahold of your life, and quick.*

I couldn't wait around to be rescued. I had to decide for myself what I wanted my life to look like, and I had to be the one who made the necessary changes. No one else, just me. Whatever needed to happen for me to be rescued, I would have to be the one to do the rescuing.

In the end, we both just knew. We knew when it was time to let go.

Tony was downstairs in the basement, where he'd been living for months. The children—Christie was seven, Bobby six, and Jackie four—were watching TV in our bedroom. I was in the kitchen, summoning my courage. Finally, I went down to the basement and found Tony sitting on the sofa. He got up, and we both just stood there, looking at each other but saying nothing, for what seemed like a very long time. I saw tears in Tony's eyes. I raised my hand and put it on his cheek.

"We have to stop this," I said. "We can't survive like this. We can't do this anymore."

Tony didn't say a word. He gathered some of his things and went upstairs and walked out the front door. I followed him and stood just outside our house, and I watched him get into his car. I could hear the sounds of the TV playing inside. I watched Tony drive away, until he disappeared around a corner.

Suddenly, the gravity of the moment hit me. *Joy, what have you done?* I thought. *How could you do this?* A thousand images flashed in my head. Me driving with Tony to look for jobs. Me and Tony opening presents under our wobbly Christmas tree. Tony bouncing Bobby on his shoulders, and Bobby laughing gleefully. All of those moments, everything we did, everything I'd dreamed of, just washed over me as I stood there in something like shock.

That reality—the reality of me and Tony—*was not my reality anymore.*

It was like I took our family photo—the photo of me and Tony and Christie and Bobby and Jackie, all of us smiling, all of us hugging, frozen forever in a portrait of happiness—and tore it to pieces. Ripped it to shreds. My children only knew Tony as their father, the man who tossed them up in the air and made them laugh. He was a hero to them, and they believed he would always be there, like the sun or the sky or the clouds. But their reality didn't matter anymore, because I took it and changed it.

I broke up our family.

I went to the bathroom and I cried really hard, and then I washed my eyes and went to the bedroom to see my children.

"Where's Daddy?" Bobby asked as soon as I walked in.

I sat down on the bed and took a deep breath.

"Okay," I said, searching for words, "I have to tell you something. Mommy and Daddy aren't going to live together anymore."

Even before I finished the sentence, Bobby cried out.

"NO, MOMMY, NO!"

He started sobbing, and I pulled him into my arms and held him tight and kept telling him everything would be okay. I pulled Christie and Jackie in and told them the same thing—everything will be fine. But they were all so little, so young and so trusting and so innocent. Not having their father in the house must have felt like the end of the world for them.

And all I could say, over and over, was *Everything will be okay.*

That night, I took the kids out for dinner and ice cream. Just the four of us. It was the start of my new mission in life, the most important one I'd ever have—to give my children the happiest, most stable lives I could possibly provide.

None of it was easy. All of it was painful. But when Tony walked out the door that night, I felt something shift inside me.

Over the next few weeks I began to sense something new bubbling up. Little sparks here and there. Little ideas and flashes and visions. A new energy. A new motivation. Inspiration. Confidence. Strength.

From the moment Tony left, I understood that I needed to become someone new.

From then on, I needed to be Joy the Courageous.

# PART
# TWO

*"JOY BEGINS THE MOMENT*
*YOU DECIDE TO DISCOVER YOURSELF."*

JOY MANGANO

# 17

In the days after Tony left, I cleaned every window, mopped every floor, washed every sheet, and organized every closet, shelf, and drawer. I dug through every cubbyhole and threw out all the clutter that had built up over the years. I wanted our home to be a reflection of our new lives. I wanted it to be clean and serene and beautiful.

That said, I couldn't afford to buy anything nice for the house. There was barely enough money to pay the bills, and none left over for new lamps or pillows or decorations or anything. My only option was to make something nice myself.

I grew up making and building things, but over the years I kind of lost touch with that side of myself.

Now, it was time to find it again.

The first thing I decided to make was a Christmas wreath. I loved Christmas and I loved wreaths, but I couldn't afford to buy a new one for the front door. Decorative wreaths were just becoming popular back then, and they were still pretty expensive.

I took the children to my local crafts store and we bought supplies—flowers, wires, ribbons, little sprigs of greenery. I went home and laid out my supplies and put the wreath together with a glue gun, piece by piece. It was fun. It felt good. After about an hour, the wreath was done, and I thought it came out beautifully—for a fraction of what a new one would have cost. I proudly hung my new wreath on the door.

But I didn't just make one for Christmas. I made one for spring, and one for summer, and one for fall. My neighbors began to notice them and ask me where I got them. I told them I made them myself.

"Can you make one for me and I'll buy it?" they started to ask.

Honestly, I didn't make the wreaths to sell them to my friends and neighbors. I was happy just to make them and give them away as gifts. But people were insistent. They wanted to buy my wreaths. Some neighbors even came with me to the crafts store and then to my home so they could watch how I made them.

Eventually, I agreed to sell my wreaths. It made me happy to see how much my neighbors loved having them. I, for one, understood how important it was to take pride in your home, and I was happy to be able to help my friends get beautiful wreaths for a price they could afford.

And that got me thinking.

What if I could turn my wreaths into a business?

I went back to the crafts store with the children, and they helped me pick out a ton of ribbons and bells and artificial flowers and other materials. I made ten new wreaths in all different styles. My mother, Toots, had worked at Bloomingdale's as a secretary for a buyer—the person who selects the products that appear in the store. She helped me arrange a meeting with him in his office. I got a sitter to stay with the children, put on my best dress, and drove into Manhattan with my wreaths wrapped up in the back of the car. I was excited and nervous and scared and hopeful all at once.

At Bloomingdale's, the buyer looked over my wreaths and frowned. He was polite, but direct.

"This is not what we do," he said. "This isn't enough product for us."

Not enough product. What did that mean? I could make more wreaths—I could make as many as he wanted! But that's not what he meant.

He meant I didn't have a line of products, or even one singularly compelling product for their customers. My product was simply not big enough for Bloomingdale's.

I drove home and put the wreaths in a closet. My idea for a wreath business never got off the ground.

But that was okay. I liked my wreaths. So did my neighbors. All of our homes were a little happier and more cheerful because of the wreaths, and that made me feel pretty good.

And you know what else?

*I was making things again.*

# 18

Something else happened around this time that had a big impact on me. Something transformative.

I joined the local Parent Teacher Association at my children's elementary school, because I wanted to be involved in their education. I met a woman named Ronni, who was president of the PTA for the entire school district. Ronni had flaming red hair and wore bright high-top sneakers with fluorescent laces. She was funny and generous and completely unique. She was also a powerhouse of positive energy. She was tireless, and was always trying to do the right thing for the schoolchildren. I was drawn to her and really liked being around her. We became really good friends.

One day, a young boy at our elementary school was riding his bicycle home and got hit by a car. He wasn't wearing a bicycle helmet, and he suffered a traumatic brain injury. When Ronni and I talked about it, we both had the same question.

*What can we do to help?*

We worked together to come up with a plan, and we reached out to local officials for support. We both saw an opportunity to do something positive for children. We called it the Heads for Helmets campaign, and our goal was getting a new bicycle helmet law passed in New York. We had door after door politely closed in our faces, but we kept pushing each other to keep going, and that's how we stayed positive. Ronni's enthusiasm was like oxygen to my flame, and mine was the same for her.

It took a while, but we persuaded local bicycle shops to donate helmets, and we raised funds to buy even more at a low cost. Then we held a huge event at Eisenhower Park in East Meadow, and we handed out free helmets to hundreds of children, including our own. Local newspapers picked up our story, and more politicians became aware of Heads for Helmets. Ronni and I were invited to go to Albany to talk to senators and congressmen about getting their support in passing a new law.

Then New York senator Norm Levy pushed the bill through the state legislature, and the New York State bicycle helmet law went into effect, requiring any bicyclist under fourteen to wear a safety-certified helmet.

I can't even begin to explain how good I felt. Literally millions of families would be helped by the law, and hopefully many lives would be saved. As a mother, it is still one of my proudest moments.

But that wasn't the only great thing to come out of that effort. There was also my remarkable new friendship with Ronni.

I grew up in a quiet household where there wasn't a lot of mutual support. Then I came out of a marriage that was the same way. I really didn't know what it was like to have someone not only support me but also push me to accomplish big things.

But that's what Ronni did for me. Being around her positive energy gave me a real charge, and she empowered me to reach higher than I would have on my own. My friendship with Ronni taught me an incredibly valuable lesson.

We are only as ambitious and capable as the people around us believe us to be.

This is one of the big keys in gaining momentum in our work and in our lives—surrounding ourselves with light, bright people.

The first step is understanding that the people we choose to have in our lives can hold us back from being our best selves—and that they can also empower us to accomplish things beyond our own abilities.

So we need to be vigilant about the people who cross into our lives. Not only are we entitled to choose who we want to be surrounded by, but it's one of the most important choices we'll ever make. To leave it to chance is just not good enough.

I think that if some people sat down and made an inventory of the meaningful people in their lives, they might be shocked at who makes the list, and how in the world they got there.

Today, I work hard to make sure I'm surrounded by light, bright people. I work just as hard to block out the negative energy of other people in my path. If someone is always putting us down or rejecting our ideas or doubting us, that's not someone we want to have in our lives.

We need to look for the light, bright people.

Something was happening. Something was stirring. It wasn't just the wreaths, or the PTA, or the helmet law.

It was me. It was how I felt inside.

I'd just blown up my old life, and I had to pick up the pieces and start my new life, and I didn't have time to sit around and try to figure it all out. I had to make something happen *now*.

I'd built new things as a child, and then I'd forgotten what it was like to build things, but now I needed to be a builder again—I needed to build new lives for myself and for my children. Christie, Bobby, and Jackie needed me to be brave. *I* needed me to be brave.

So whatever new life I was going to create, I had to start creating it right away.

# 19

I didn't have money to take family vacations, so in the summers I'd sometimes take the children to spend a night or two on Rudy's sailboat. He named it *Camelot*, because that sounded like the name of a boat rich people would own.

My father wasn't really a sailor. I think he took to boats because it made him feel debonair and worldly. He liked the idea of owning a boat, even if it wasn't a very big one. Every time we went on the *Camelot* he proudly talked to us about boat things, like his fancy new twin engine or the jib boom or his new navigation goggles.

The funny thing is, we never really went sailing all that much. I can remember only a couple of times when my father actually took us out to sea. Usually, we just drove to the marina where the boat was docked and scampered aboard so the children could sleep on it overnight, which they loved doing.

One breezy summer day, my father invited all of us out on the *Camelot*. His new girlfriend, Thelma, was there. Thelma dressed mainly in stylish black slacks and shirts, which to me gave off the look of old money. She was nice enough to the children, but a little standoffish with me. Rudy seemed to like her. She'd been married before, to a businessman who manufactured something that made him very wealthy. When he passed, Thelma inherited his fortune, and I'm sure that part of it appealed to my father. But in those days, Rudy dated a lot of different women. We never knew how long his girlfriends would be around.

That afternoon, one of the kids spilled something on the teak-wood floor of the *Camelot*'s deck. I knew my father was meticulous about his boat, so I jumped up and grabbed the mop to clean up the spill.

The boat mop—or navy mop, as it was called—was a clunky thing. You swabbed the decks with it and then you wrung it out by squeezing the cotton strands with your hands over the side of the boat. It wasn't a very pleasant task, but I was used to it, because I did the same thing with my cotton mops at home. I didn't use the sponge mops that were available back then, because they just didn't work that well for me. I used an old-fashioned cotton mop instead, which meant I had to wring out the dirty water with my hands.

But on that day, while I was cleaning up the spill and squeezing out the cotton mop head, a very clear thought popped into my head. Out of nowhere, and in the form of a question.

*There has to be a better way, doesn't there?*

There's a way of thinking in the business world that says for an idea to be worth paying attention to, it has to be huge and complicated, like the airplane, or the computer, or the iPhone. These are the kinds of monumental ideas that truly change people's lives, the thinking goes, so these are the ideas that are truly worthy of your passion and time.

But that's simply not true.

Look at the cup holder in your car. Someone dreamed that up. Someone had the idea to create a little cylinder to hold your cup while you drive. That's not a monumental idea, but it matters. It makes a real difference. Imagine driving three hours without having a place to put your hot cup of coffee. We take it for granted now, but someone's idea for car cup holders improved millions of lives in a very real way.

The same is true in our personal lives. Sometimes we need to make big changes, like I did when I split up with Tony. But sometimes the smallest change can improve our lives in powerful ways. We don't have to think in terms of making sweeping changes, as if that's the only way we can accomplish anything meaningful in our lives.

Put simply, small ideas can change lives. A simple solution to a common problem. A better way of doing something you do every day.

In business, and in life, a little can be a lot.

That day on my father's boat, I finished cleaning up the spill and put the navy mop away. But I couldn't get the thought of a better mop out of my mind. When we went home the next day, it was still there, buzzing around in my brain. A week later, it was all I could think about.

So finally one night, after having dinner and clearing the dishes and putting the children to bed, I sat down at the kitchen table by myself, took out my pencil and my sketchbook, and started drawing mops.

# 20

Even then, I understood that most people didn't really care about mops. Mops were just there, and you used them and forgot about them. Mops worked well enough. Mops were boring.

But I couldn't shake the feeling that mops could work *better*.

I thought about the problems with my old-fashioned cotton mops. The main issue was wringing them out. The only way to do it was with our hands, which meant we had to use rubber gloves or else we'd end up with dirt and harsh chemicals on our fingers. It also meant bending over to wring them out, which wasn't easy for people with bad backs. And the more we used them, the filthier and moldier they became, until we finally had to throw them away.

I started fooling around with the basic structure of a mop. I found a broom at home and unscrewed the broom part so I had a plain stick. Then I attached cotton strands to one end with the hot glue I had used to make my wreaths. Then I took a cardboard toilet paper roll and slipped it down the handle of the mop. Why? Because I wanted to see if there was a way I could squeeze the mop head with something other than my hands—like the toilet paper roll.

I drew up a lot of sketches, trying to figure it out. If I could find a way to make the roll spin around the stick while connected to the cotton strings, then I could make the mop strings twist together and tighten around themselves, which would wring out all the water—without me having to touch the mop head at all.

If I could do that, I would have a self-wringing mop.

So I drew more sketches. I drew *hundreds* of sketches. I realized that if I could make the mop head one long, continuous strand of cotton that was looped back and forth around an attachment on the handle, then I could twist the handle to make the cotton tighten and squeeze, which would wring out the water. And if I used a lot of cotton—one of the most absorbent materials there is—I could create a dense cluster of strands that would do a much better job than sponge mops.

And what if I made the cotton mop head detachable, so you could throw it in the washing machine dirty, and it could come out clean?

Piece by piece, it started to come together. It started to make sense. The crude prototype I created with a broom handle and a toilet paper roll wasn't functional, but it was enough to make me reach a decision:

*You know what? I want to do something with this.*

But what, exactly, was I supposed to do?

After Tony left, my finances weren't great. I took a part-time job as a hostess in a fancy restaurant in Glen Cove, which helped supplement the child-support checks I received from Tony. My father had moved on from his bus company and opened an auto body shop in Deer Park, and I did some accounting work for him, and in return he helped me out whenever he could. And when things got really tight, which was often, I cashed in a couple of savings bonds.

But money was always scarce, and every week I had to scratch out enough to pay the bills. There wasn't any left over for the first thing I had to do with my mop idea—run a patent search to make sure no one else had had the idea first. There was only one person I could turn to for help.

My father.

"This is what I've been working on," I told Rudy one day, handing over my sketches and prototype. "I want to patent it."

"You want to what?"

"I want to patent it," I said. "I'm going to follow through on this."

"Okay," my father said.

"Do you know a lawyer?" I asked.

"Sure. I'll take care of it."

My father had his attorney do a search of existing patents. I thought I was on safe ground, because my idea seemed so original and specific to me. A few days later, the attorney called Rudy and told him the results of the search.

"You can't patent this," the attorney said.

"Why not?"

"Because someone already has the patent."

When my father told me that, I was crushed. I couldn't believe it was true. A large company in Australia apparently *had* come up with the same idea. I found the number for the company's US representative, Eddie Arnolds, who seemed to handle all sorts of different things for them, including patent licensing and book publishing. I called him and asked him to send me a copy of the patent and one of the mops.

When it arrived, I tore open the packaging to get a look at it. The mop was made of a metal tube, and the mop strings got pulled inside the handle to wring them out. It didn't look anything like my self-wringing navy mop, but it *was* a self-wringing mop. The fact that it existed at all was devastating. What was I supposed to do now?

"You can't make the mop," my father warned me. "Now that we've contacted Eddie and he sent us his mop, you can't make your mop."

I thought about that for a few seconds.

Then I said, "No, you're wrong. I can still make my mop."

# 21

To his credit, my father knew my idea was good. So he agreed to call Eddie back, and together they worked out a deal.

We would create and sell my version of the mop, and the Australian company would get money, or a royalty, for every mop we sold. Part of the deal was that we would use Eddie's manufacturing partner, a California-based group called West Coast Molds & Manufacturing, to make the plastic molds we needed to manufacture the mop.

Now all I had to do was come up with the money to make the molds. At the time, I had about $2,000 in my checking account.

I sat down with my father to talk about the next step.

"Don't worry about it," is all he said. "I'll take care of it."

Honestly, I didn't think to ask him where the money was coming from. I was okay with letting Rudy pay West Coast to make the molds, and with letting him handle the finances. It wasn't like I had a lot of options.

I booked a flight to California to supervise the creation of the molds at the West Coast factory. I didn't know anything about industrial molds, so I read everything I could find to gain a solid understanding of how they worked. I took Christie, Bobby, and Jackie with me to California, because I wanted them to feel like they were on this journey with me.

In California, I met with Bill, the chief engineer and owner of West Coast. Eddie Arnolds was there, too. Bill was friendly and accommodating, and he even invited me to his house for a family dinner. Once the pleasantries were done, we sat down and looked over the molds they'd built based on my sketches.

Immediately, I could tell they were all wrong. They didn't sync up with the sketches. On top of that, the mop heads were a problem. I wanted a certain amount of cotton in every mop head, which meant we needed to create a special loom to manufacture the heads, and the engineers were having trouble with it.

I tried to be as precise as I could, but in the end I had to design and develop the loom myself, with the help of one of the mechanics at my father's shop.

It took several months, but they finally got the molds right, which meant we could start making the mop heads. Not much later, West Coast sent me three fully manufactured mops to test.

When the big package arrived at my house, I sat down and stared at it for a while before opening it. I felt nervous and excited. Inside that box was my idea—my idea *come to life*. I had never gotten this far with my flea collar, but I learned from my mistake, and now here I was. I looked at the box until I couldn't look at it any longer, and then I ripped it open.

I pulled out one of the mops and held it in my hands. It was beautiful. The bright-white cotton mop head; the sleek, movable cylinder; the lightweight red plastic handle—it all came together to create something simple and clean and functional.

Something that was *real*.

I took the mops into my bedroom and put them on my bed, and I sat down next to them and stared at them some more. I knew what I had to do next. I took the mops to the kitchen to try them out. I got out a bucket and put water on the floor and soaked it up, and I twisted the cylinder around the handle and wrung the mop head into the bucket. It worked perfectly. I tried it again, and it worked perfectly again. I tried it a few more times, and it worked every time.

I just didn't want to stop mopping.

Then Christie came into the kitchen, and Bobby and Jackie followed her, and the kids each grabbed a mop and started mopping with me. They weren't even as tall as the mops, but they did their best. They were giggling and I was giggling, except I was also crying at the same time. The four of us spent the next twenty minutes happily mopping up a kitchen floor that wasn't even dirty.

That night I took Christie, Bobby, and Jackie out for ice cream. I wanted to celebrate the moment. I knew full well that I was in debt and that I hadn't sold a single mop. But I didn't care.

I wanted to celebrate anyway.

There's a myth in the business world that says we shouldn't stop to celebrate until we cross the finish line. We should keep our heads down and keep our focus on the end goal and pay attention to nothing else until we've accomplished everything we set out to do, or else we'll risk losing our focus and failing.

But that just never felt right to me.

I believe no success is too small to celebrate. The journey to create something meaningful is too long and too hard and too unpredictable for us to celebrate only when we reach the finish line. We have to find little victories for ourselves along the way so we can keep ourselves motivated and excited about what comes next.

These little celebrations are the fuel that keeps us going. Deciding to deny ourselves a little satisfaction along the way will stop us before we really even get started.

That's why I took the children out for ice cream that wonderful night—so we could celebrate the birth of my brand-new mop.

I already had a name for it. I called it the Marine Mop.

# 22

West Coast sent us more mops, and I scrounged up enough money to buy a three-foot-by-three-foot square of clear fiberglass—my portable floor—from the hardware store. Then I took the Marine Mop to every boat show, flea market, and county fair I could find.

Ronni, who loved my mop idea and offered to help, came along, and most of the time I took my children with me, too. I wanted to involve them in the project as much as I could, so they'd understand what their mother was working on for all those hours every night. And besides, they loved any kind of show or fair. To them, everything was a carnival.

"Come on, guys, let's go!" I'd tell them. "It's gonna be fun!"

At the boat shows, Ronni and I demonstrated the Marine Mop nonstop. We'd show people how easy it was to use, and sometimes Christie or Bobby would jump in and wring it out, too.

"It's so easy to use, even *I* can do it," Bobby would say.

Almost everyone who watched us use the mop said something like "Wow, that is amazing" or "What a great idea."

Then they asked how much it cost.

The Marine Mop was $19.99, or roughly four times the average price of an ordinary mop.

"But this mop is so much better than other mops, it's the last mop you'll ever have to buy!" I'd tell them.

Some people thought the price was too high, but just about everyone *loved* the idea of the mop. After a few weeks of going to shows and fairs, we'd sold about a dozen Marine Mops.

That might not seem like a whole lot to some people, but to me, twelve mops was a *lot* of mops.

That was twelve people who'd now have a much easier time cleaning their homes. Twelve people whose lives I'd helped improve in a small but meaningful way. To me, that felt like a real achievement—a success worth celebrating.

Selling twelve mops gave me the fuel I needed to keep going.

Most of the people who attended the boat shows were sailing enthusiasts who brought their sons and wives and business partners with them. They were all curious about the mop, but the people who tended to get most excited by it were women like me. I noticed that a lot of them were saying the same thing.

"Boy, I wish I had one of these in my kitchen," they'd say.

"Yeah, me, too," I'd reply.

You might be thinking, *Well, yeah, Joy, that's pretty obvious, how could you not get it?* All I can say is, back then, my only plan was to help people clean their boats, and I was completely focused on that. But after a trade show where three women in a row said the same thing—"I want this in my kitchen"—the light bulb went off. (*See, I finally got it!*)

As usual, the idea came in the form of a question.

*Wait a minute, why* can't *this mop work in the kitchen?*

That night I cooked dinner for the children and put them to bed, and then I sat down to rest my tired feet. But my mind just wouldn't shut off. Turning the Marine Mop into a kitchen mop would mean expanding from the relatively small boating industry to one of the biggest industries of all—home goods. And that meant my little idea wouldn't be so little anymore. It had the potential to be a really *big* idea.

I sat down at the kitchen table and pulled out my notebook and started writing down new names.

Some people will have you believe that in order to create anything meaningful and successful, you have to take enormous risks—quit your job, sell your house, clean out your savings, upend your life.

Basically, you have to jump off a cliff.

But that's not true. Look at me. I didn't jump off any cliff. I took some risks, and some of them were scary, but I didn't completely upend my life. I took the children with me to demonstrations, and at night I still cooked them dinner and tucked them into bed. Getting started with my mop idea didn't change my new life all that much.

The truth is that you don't have to risk everything to get started. Starting anything, even something big, doesn't have to be an all-or-nothing proposition, financially or time-wise. We just need to take the first step, and the next, and be willing to see where those steps may lead us.

That night at the kitchen table, I wrote down about thirty different names for the mop, until I finally settled on the one I really loved.

And that is when the Marine Mop became the *Miracle* Mop.

# 23

Gunshots rang through the air, one after another. *Bang bang bang bang bang*. Really loud blasts, coming from just a few feet away. It wasn't a gun battle or anything like that. It was just my neighbors having fun.

You see, I set up a little office in the back room of my father's auto body shop to use for my new mop business. The room was adjacent to the back alley of the next-door welding business. It just so happened that in their free time, the welders liked to use the alley for target practice with their guns and rifles.

Yes, my first office was right next to an illegal shooting range.

That wasn't the only problem. The back room was where my father's mechanics usually had lunch, and they weren't thrilled about getting the boot. The room was also a mess. There were two sheet-metal desks and an adding machine, and that was it. The floor was covered with dirt and broken glass, and the walls were plastered with pictures of naked girls. The first thing I did was start ripping the pictures off the walls.

That's when Richie, the shop's head mechanic, walked over and gave me a dirty look.

"I'm sorry, but I have to do this," I explained. "My kids are going to be coming in here."

Richie didn't seem impressed.

"Just don't touch the ones in the bathroom," he said.

Ronni and I got some new lamps and a rug from a nearby flea market, and we fixed up the room as best we could on a microbudget. In the end, we probably spent more money on cleaning supplies than we did on office supplies.

Then it was time to get back on the road. We loaded twenty Miracle Mops in the back of my old white Lumina minivan, and we drove to every hardware store in a fifty-mile radius. We drove west toward Manhattan and east out to Montauk, north to the Long Island Sound and south toward the Great South Bay.

Two moms in a minivan, lugging mops into hardware stores. Nothing crazy about that, is there?

Nearly every store owner told us they couldn't sell a $20 mop.

"Who's going to pay that for a mop?" most of them asked.

But not all of them.

We convinced one store owner to stock a grand total of five Miracle Mops. A few days later, when we came back, he told us he'd sold two of them.

Two mops sold. Two out of five. To me, that wasn't bad news.

It was *great* news.

It meant at least two more people in the world didn't think $20 was too much to pay for a better mop. Selling two mops was a cause for celebration! Remember I said to celebrate the small successes? Well, if selling a grand total of two whole mops isn't a small success, I don't know what is.

Still, I knew I needed to find a way to sell more mops.

I had the idea to approach the buyers at Amway—the company behind the giant catalog that sold everything from home products to jewelry to home insurance. I set up the call, and I let Ronni do the talking. Ronni was simply better than I was at that stuff. She could talk her way out of a sealed box. To me, she was our best hope of convincing Amway to put the Miracle Mop in their catalog.

And she did it!

Amway agreed to list the mop in its catalog. That was a *major* victory, and it exposed the Miracle Mop to many tens of thousands of people, not just a handful here and there. We just had to hope that people understood from the catalog that the Miracle Mop was truly something new and special that could make a real difference in their lives.

And you know what? They did.

Over time, *hundreds* of people bought the Miracle Mop. Not two or ten or twenty—hundreds! I was ecstatic! We also kept adding hardware stores to our roster of clients, one here, one there, and every month we sold a few more mops than we had the previous month.

We were heading in the right direction.

My next fixation was Kmart.

At the time, Kmart was *the* retail giant, with stores in forty-nine states, plus Mexico and Canada. I was convinced that if I could get the Miracle Mop into Kmart, we'd be set for life. I wrote a letter to a chief buyer in the cleaning category. I put a lot of thought into the letter and filled it with as much passion and confidence as I could summon. Then I waited.

But the buyer didn't respond.

So I wrote another letter. And another one. And another one after that. I probably wrote ten in all. Finally, after weeks of being pestered, the buyer agreed to see me, probably just to make me go away.

Success!

Ronni and I met with the buyer—a handsome, distinguished man with silver hair—in his office at the company's headquarters in Troy, Michigan. I got ready to demonstrate how the Miracle Mop worked, but the buyer's mouth twisted into a frown, and he stopped me before I could even get started.

"I'm sorry, but our mops are $4.99," he said. "I can't sell a mop for $20."

"You can if the people see how it works," I said. "I'm telling you. When I show people how this works, they love it. They can't believe it. It really helps them, and it's the last mop they'll ever have to buy."

We went back and forth like that for a while. The buyer simply couldn't understand why selling a mop that didn't need to be replaced was a *good* thing. The conventional approach was to create a product that kept consumers coming back to buy another one, again and again. Why sell consumers just one mop, he asked, when you can sell them a mop that doesn't last so they have to keep buying more?

To me, that was just crazy. I argued that consumers would love the Miracle Mop because, unlike any other similar product, it gave them what they really needed in a mop—ease of use, reliability, no hand-wringing, less time cleaning.

It was a battle of wills between the buyer and me, but I didn't give up until I'd finally made a dent in his way of thinking.

"Okay, okay," he relented. "Why don't you demonstrate it in one of my stores, and let's see how the customers react to it."

Success again!

A few weeks later, Ronni and I were back in Troy with a batch of Miracle Mops. The buyer set us up in the cleaning section of a local Kmart. I'd asked Richie from my father's auto body shop to make us a square patch of black-and-white linoleum, and Ronni and I used that for our demonstrations instead of the fiberglass, because it looked more like what you'd see in an actual kitchen. We had two buckets and two mops, and, starting early in the morning, Ronni and I demonstrated the mop for every customer who walked by.

It was a long, long day. Ronni and I did so many demonstrations that our hands were bruised and red and raw. By the end of the day my feet hurt so much that I asked Ronni to grab me a pair of slippers from a nearby aisle so I could get out of my shoes.

But that was okay, because the demonstrations went well. They went *really* well. People *loved* the Miracle Mop, and we sold a few hundred mops that day. The buyer dropped by and noticed the customers' enthusiasm. He told us he would call in a few days.

Ronni and I walked out of the store, both of us exhausted, me in my new slippers, and we did a little happy dance in the parking lot.

I'd told the buyer I wanted the Miracle Mop to be sold in every Kmart in the country. But to be honest, I didn't know if that was possible. Back then, Kmart already sold mops from two giant companies, each with a line of many different mops, as well as hundreds of other stick-good products. And there I was with my one little mop. I had no idea what the buyer had in mind for us. Maybe he'd put us in a few stores to see how well we sold.

We waited for days. And days and days and days. And then, finally, the phone rang.

"Here's what we're going to do," the buyer said. "We'll sell the mop in every Kmart east of the Mississippi. Then we'll compare it to the other mops and see how you stack up."

Wait a minute—did he say every Kmart east of the Mississippi? Did I hear that right? Hundreds of stores????

I'd heard it right. The Miracle Mop was going to be sold in *twenty-six states!* More than half the states in the country! I hung up with the buyer and immediately made another call.

"Ronni!" I screamed. "You're not going to believe this!"

In my meeting with the Kmart buyer, the first thing he said to me— after saying hello—was *no*.

Not *maybe* or *we'll see*—just *no*. A flat *no*. He didn't even let me get to the demonstration. His answer, he told me, was *no*.

But by the end of the meeting, his answer wasn't *no* anymore.

Here's the point: we shouldn't be afraid of hearing *no*, because *no* is not the end of the world. There are many, many options after getting a *no*.

We can argue and turn the *no* into a *yes*, like I did with the buyer. Or we can rework our idea to eventually get to a *yes*. Or we can go to someone else and get *them* to say *yes*. As Ronni and I would always say, over, under, around, or through. There are an infinite number of options available to us after we hear the word *no*.

The only unacceptable option is giving up.

Throughout my career, I've felt like I got told *no* a million times a day, and I'm not exaggerating that much. Even today, I get told *no* all the time. I hear *no* way more often than I hear *yes*. That's just a fact of life and business that I have to deal with.

But remember—it takes only one *yes* to get things moving.

A *no* is productive! It's a starting point! It's a chance for us to learn something (Why did he say *no*?), reset our thinking (Do I need to describe

110

this differently?), draw motivation (I'll show him!), and become stronger. A *no* translates into raw energy that will power us forward.

As long as we know that a *no* is never a *no*.

Not long after we got into Kmart, someone told me about another big retail outlet that might be a good place for the Miracle Mop.

I'd never heard of it, so I did some research. It was a relatively new concept, unlike anything else in the retail world. It was designed to bring products directly into the homes of millions of customers at a time using the power of TV, and it represented the future of retail marketing and sales. I was more than interested in it. I became obsessed with it. It became my new mission to sell the Miracle Mop through this new company.

The company was called QVC.

# 24

In 1977, a man named Bud Paxson was managing a small radio station in Clearwater, Florida. Paxson made money by selling airtime on his station to advertisers who wanted to reach his listeners. One of the station's advertisers sold can openers. When the advertiser couldn't afford to pay for an ad with money, he sent Paxson 112 can openers instead.

Paxson had one of the station's talk show hosts try to sell the can openers on the air, hoping to get rid of a few of them that way. The host simply told listeners to drive down to the station, hand over the money, and drive away with a can opener, if they wanted one.

Within an hour, all 112 can openers had been sold.

Five years later, Paxson and a partner launched the Home Shopping Club, which later became the Home Shopping Network, and which today is known as HSN.

It was the birth of the electronic retailing industry.

In 1986, QVC became the second home shopping network. The first product sold on air at QVC was a shower radio.

The next year, QVC set a record for first-full-year fiscal sales for a new public company, and a new retail rivalry began—HSN vs. QVC.

I read everything I could find about QVC, and I came across the name of one of their buyers for cleaning products, a woman named Cindy. A letter and a phone call later, I had an appointment to meet with Cindy in her office in West Chester, Pennsylvania.

Back in those days, QVC was a company dominated by men. A lot of the management team came out of traditional retail institutions like Macy's and Bloomingdale's, and they were mostly men who had their own, old-world way of doing things. One of them, an executive named Dan Hardy, developed the network's guiding principle in its early days.

"I just believe in telling great stories," he told one new management employee, "and I will keep telling those great stories, and you will have to prove to me that anything new you bring to me is more valuable than what I already have on the air."

In other words, I would have to find a way to impress QVC's established old guard if I was going to get anywhere with my mop.

Luckily, my first meeting was with one of the few female buyers working at QVC in those days. Ronni and I did our demonstration for Cindy in her office, and it took her only a few minutes to reach a decision.

"I'll take 5,000 of them," she said.

I looked at Ronni, and Ronni looked at me. I guess we both wanted to be sure we had heard what we heard.

We were used to getting orders for a few hundred mops here and there, but 5,000 mops? *Five thousand mops?*

That moment was utterly thrilling, *and* utterly frightening.

For one thing, going back to our manufacturer in California and having them make 5,000 mops in a short amount of time would cost a lot of money up front—money I didn't have.

But there was another catch, and it involved the QVC business model.

Cindy wasn't really *buying* 5,000 mops from us. She was only ordering them. No one at QVC could ever be sure how many units of any product would sell, but they always stocked as many as they'd sell if the product was a hit—in my case, 5,000 mops. Cindy couldn't order just 100 mops to see how they fared. She had to order 5,000 and believe they would all get sold over time.

And if they didn't?

Well, that wasn't Cindy's problem. All she had to do was return the unsold mops to me. And once they came back to me, they would be *my* problem. If the QVC debut didn't go well, I could end up saddled with thousands of mops and no place to sell them.

But no—I couldn't think that way. I had to stay positive and pour all my energy into getting the mops made.

I told my father about our meeting at QVC and the order for 5,000 mops. Rudy saw dollar signs.

"Don't worry about the money," he said. "I'll take care of it."

We had about two months to get 5,000 Miracle Mops created, packaged, and shipped. I called the engineer at West Coast Molds & Manufacturing, and he said they could do it. Perfect! I stayed in contact with Cindy at QVC, who handled everything regarding the mop. All I knew for sure was that QVC's top salesman—the network's first-ever on-air host—was going to be the one to sell the mop on air. Cindy promised me I was in great hands.

Finally, the big day arrived. The Miracle Mop was debuting on QVC. I gathered everyone in the living room of my house—Christie, Bobby, and Jackie; Rudy and Thelma; and Ronni. Everyone huddled together on or around the sofa, except for me.

I was way too nervous to sit down.

Instead I paced back and forth from the kitchen to the living room, my heart beating wildly. Whatever happened in the next fifteen minutes would probably shape the rest of my life, one way or the other. Ronni told me to sit down and relax. But I just couldn't.

And then—it was time.

We all hushed each other and stared at my small TV as the friendly face of the segment's host appeared.

"We have an exciting new product to show you," he said, or at least that's what I think he said. My focus wasn't on the host, or what he was saying.

It was on where he was standing.

He was in a garage. Next to him, some guy was standing next to a big bucket and holding the Miracle Mop. None of it made sense to me. Why a garage? Why a guy?

But okay—they know what they're doing, right?

The host talked about the Miracle Mop while the guy cleaned up a spill on the floor and tried to wring out the mop head. His movements were awkward, almost as if it was the first time he'd ever held the mop in his hands. He didn't wring it out properly or do anything to convey how easy it was to use.

But even worse, the host wasn't talking about the mop the way I *thought* about the mop.

He didn't say how it would cut down on the time we spent mopping and cleaning, or how it would help those of us with bad backs, or how we wouldn't need to put on gloves to wring out the mops with our hands, or how we could detach the mop head and put it in the washing machine, or any of the other reasons I made the mop in the first place!

The host didn't say any of that. He didn't talk about how the Miracle Mop helped people like me.

I slumped down on the arm of the sofa and felt the terrible silence in my living room as we all grappled to understand what was happening.

"It's bombing," my father finally said. "It's dying up there."

He was right. The segment was awkward and lifeless. All of a sudden, the QVC cameras cut away to another product. The segment ended before the allotted fifteen minutes were up. The host moved on to whatever was next as if the Miracle Mop had never even existed. Everyone looked at me to see my reaction, and I felt my face turn red.

"Joy, this is not good," my father said. "This is really bad."

That night, I didn't sleep at all. Not a single minute. I tossed and turned and went over everything that happened in my head. Bright and early the next day I called Cindy at QVC, and she picked up right away.

"They didn't sell it right!" I yelled into the phone. "They didn't talk about the features, and they didn't even wring it out the right way!"

"This happens sometimes," Cindy calmly said.

"Okay, okay," I said. "What's next? What are we going to do now?"

"Joy, the mops are Return to Vendor," she said.

"Return to Vendor? What does that even mean?"

"Return to Vendor. You're the vendor. They get returned to you."

I couldn't breathe. I was furious. This couldn't be happening. It was the worst-case scenario. It was worse than the worst-case scenario.

That night on QVC, they sold a total of 500 Miracle Mops over two abbreviated airings.

Which meant 4,500 mops were headed back to me.

Which meant that I was in big, big trouble.

# 25

The next day, I called Cindy again. She didn't respond.

I wrote her letters, and she didn't answer them.

I wrote letters to other people at QVC, but I never heard back. Nothing worked. No one wanted to talk to me. As far as QVC was concerned, it was a done deal. The Miracle Mop was a failure. End of story.

But I couldn't accept that. That wasn't an option for me. I couldn't do nothing. I had to do something. I had to find a way to do *something*.

I had to find someone higher up than Cindy and convince him to give the Miracle Mop another chance.

So I got into my old minivan and drove the three hours to West Chester, Pennsylvania, and walked into the lobby of QVC.

I didn't have an appointment. I just asked to see Dan Hardy, an executive vice president—and Cindy's boss. The receptionist told me to have a seat. I sat in the lobby for the next several hours before someone finally came to show me in.

A QVC staffer took me up in the elevator to Dan's floor and walked me through a glass door into a small, dark conference room.

In the middle of the room, six men sat around a big table. No women, just men.

All six of the men looked up at me when I walked in. I could feel every one of their eyeballs on me as I stood there. My legs felt weak.

Then Cindy came into the room right behind me. At the head of the table, a man stood up. It was Dan Hardy.

"Okay, Joy," he said, "you wanted to talk about your mop, go ahead and talk about your mop."

"The show was all wrong," I blurted out. "You did it all wrong."

"Cindy, what happened with the mop?" Dan asked.

"It's in RTV status," Cindy said. "It didn't sell through."

"No, no, wait a minute," I said. "You had a guy in a garage trying to sell it! He didn't even know how to use it! When I go to boat shows and flea markets and Kmart, everyone loves the mop. Everyone walks away with the mop!"

Dan just listened. The rest of the men kept staring.

"They *get* it," I said. "The people get it. They understand how the mop can help make their lives better. You didn't talk about how it saves your hands and saves your back, or about how the mop head comes off. You didn't talk about how you can wash it in the washing machine so it's germ-free. Here, let me show you."

I grabbed the mop that had I brought with me and began a demonstration, just like I'd done a thousand times at boat shows. And I didn't stop talking, not for a second. I talked about all the reasons I made the mop in the first place, and why women like me needed it in their homes. Showing and talking, showing and talking. Just keep going, Joy.

Out of the corner of my eye I saw one of the men at the table hand a folded-up note to Dan. Dan read the note, folded it back up, and put it in his pocket. I didn't know what was going on, but I kept talking.

"Okay," Dan finally said, putting up his hand to stop me. "Here's what we'll do. Cindy, don't return the mops."

Cindy scowled. Then Dan turned to face me.

"Joy, we're going to put you on the air to sell the mops. If they don't sell, they're going back to you."

And that was it.

I walked out of the conference room in a kind of daze. I had gotten my second chance, and I should have been elated, but I wasn't. All I could think about was what Dan said.

*Joy, we're going to put you on the air.*

I never asked to go on the air. I just said that when I talked about the mops, people understood why they were unique. But now I was going on the air. I was going to talk about my mop on live TV. I was going to be beamed into *90 million homes*.

And the one thing I hated more than anything else was public speaking.

How did this happen?

It was only much later that Dan told me what was written on that note.

Five simple words.

*Get her out of here.*

# 26

"You did what!?!?" Ronni said when I called her with the news. "You told them you would go on air??"

"I didn't tell them, they told me!"

We both knew Ronni was better suited to do an on-air demonstration. She was the extrovert. She was the ball of energy. But she couldn't be the one to go on the air. It had to be me. It was my mop, and I had to be the one to talk about it. Even if the thought of being on TV made me sick.

Ronni and I practiced the demonstration over and over. I made sure that this time the segment would be on a kitchen set, and Ronni and I bought several buckets that were perfectly color-coordinated. I knew all the benefits of the mop by heart and could recite them in my sleep, because they weren't just talking points to me—everything I said about the Miracle Mop represented my deeply held belief that it would make people's lives better. I wasn't speaking from a script.

I was speaking from my heart.

Early one fall morning, Ronni, the children, and I set out in my old Lumina. We drove down into New Jersey, and then on through Amish country in southern Pennsylvania. We even saw a couple of horse-drawn buggies. And then we were there, in scenic West Chester—site of the studios of QVC.

The facility was an imposing place. It was enormous. Lots of people running around, lots of thick black cables on the floor, lots of energy and activity. In the middle of it all there was an enormous circular platform, about the size of my whole house, that was broken into four separate stages, like pie wedges. The platform slowly rotated so that different sets faced a large bank of lights and cameras at different times. One of the sets was a living room. One of them was a bedroom. And one of them—the set I'd be on—was a kitchen.

Ronni and the kids sat with me in the greenroom while I got ready for the show. A stylist touched up my hair and makeup. I had the option to wear a fancy, glamorous dress, but I went with slacks and a simple top instead. Getting dressed up to mop a kitchen floor didn't make much sense to me.

Then a staffer with a clipboard came into the greenroom and told me it was time to go. I hugged Ronni and gave Christie, Bobby, and Jackie each one last quick kiss.

"Good luck, Mommy," they all shouted as I left.

The staffer walked me through the long narrow hallways until we arrived at the backstage area behind the rotating platform. The on-air host that day—the host I would do the show with—was the same one who had hosted the first, disastrous Miracle Mop segment. He was already there when I arrived, and he nodded at me but didn't say anything. He didn't seem too happy to have to talk about the mop again.

A familiar feeling swept over me—the feeling of being out of my element. Of being inferior. After all, regular people didn't sell products on QVC. Professional hosts and TV people and models sold products. Yet there I was, a single mom from Long Island with no TV experience and a fear of public speaking, about to do God knows what in front of millions and millions of people.

I couldn't have been farther from my comfort zone.

But that was okay, I told myself. It didn't matter what anyone thought about me, or if they expected me to embarrass myself on TV. It only mattered that I believed in myself. So I closed my eyes and blocked out everything and focused on what I had to do. Focused on the single next step of my journey. And it worked. Doing that worked. I felt calmer. Then I felt stronger. I felt my energy start to build. Standing backstage, I felt something deep inside me begin to rise to the surface.

"Let's get you on the set," a producer said.

I took a deep breath and walked into the makeshift kitchen. Earlier, Ronni and I had carefully placed our buckets and mops just where we wanted them on the set, and there they were, waiting for me. I picked up the mop and held it tightly. I heard someone yell out a word.

"Rotate!"

The enormous platform started to move. Slowly. Very slowly. Inch by inch. It was rotating in the direction of the live TV cameras. I stood there, holding my mop, waiting. I could feel my heart pounding in my chest. Actually, I could *hear* it pounding in my ears. I told myself to breathe and tried to take deep breaths, but all I could manage were short, shallow ones. My lungs didn't want to open. The stage kept moving, slowly, slowly. It felt like forever.

And then it stopped.

Me with Duke,
eleven years old.

Toots on a ski trip in
Stowe, Vermont.

Me bringing in birthday cake for twins Tony and Susette.
This was after we'd all graduated college.

Tony singing at
our wedding.

Tony and me at
our wedding.

Me in my uniform when I worked at Eastern Airlines.

Ronny Lee with Tony when we brought
Christie home from the hospital.

Left to right: Bobby, Jackie, our dog Champ, Christie.

Bobby, Jackie, and Christie posing for a holiday photo with one of my wreaths in the background.

Us visiting
Tony's office at
Wise Foods.

Tony and the
children with
Rudy on his
sailboat.

The children
at our house in
East Meadow,
waiting for Tony.

Me and Ronni
demonstrating at Kmart.

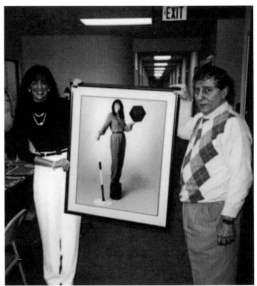

Me and Rudy holding my holiday
gift from our office staff.

Photo taken during the
filming of the Miracle
Mop infomercial.

Me on the QVC stage for the debut of the Piatto Bakery Box.

Ronni, myself, and Jan in the QVC greenroom.

*Clockwise:*

My youngest daughter, Jackie, and Sean on vacation in Italy.

My oldest daughter, Christie, with her husband, Matt, at a movie premiere.

My son, Bobby, and his wife, Theo, at their rehearsal dinner in Hawaii.

Giving the commencement speech at Pace University, 2016.

Receiving an honorary doctorate degree from Pace University, 2016.

In my offices with my three children, 2016.

In my factory warehouse, 2016.

Filming the *Meet Joy* series in Columbus Circle, NYC.

At my desk on any given day!

On set at HSN for the Huggable Hanger 20th Anniversary show, 2017.

Filming for Macy's, 2016.

With Jennifer Lawrence and Bradley Cooper at the *JOY* premiere.

Matt, Christie, Sean, Jackie, Me, Theo, and Bobby at the premiere for *JOY*.

Christie, me, Jackie, and Bobby at the movie premiere.

Filming product for
HSN at my home.

Filming for the Huggable
Hangers commercial.

Filming the commercial for the retail launch.

Tufftech Luggage with new SpinBall wheels.

HSN program guide cover for the launch of my Tufftech Luggage.

Me on the February 2016 issue of *Good Housekeeping* magazine.

*Top to bottom:*

On a boat with my beautiful
dog, Baby, in 2014. She
is a Japanese Spitz.

Tony with Toots after a holiday
meal in 2005 at my present home.

At home in the kitchen with
Christie, Bobby, and Jackie.

In my living room with my new
loves, grandchildren Alexandria
and Christopher, in 2017.

The kitchen set was now facing all the heavy lights hanging off the ceiling, and it was brightly lit up. Three big cameras pointed straight at me. Lots of people stood around behind the cameras—technicians, producers, assistants. About 200 telephone operators sat at tables off to the side. I noticed Dan standing nearby, leaning against the wall with his arms crossed in front of him. He gave me a smile that looked like a "go get 'em" smile.

A thought pushed its way to the front of my mind.

*Everything is at stake, Joy. Right here, right now. This very second.*

Then I heard the host's cheerful voice.

"Well, look who's here," he announced to the TV audience. "It's Joy. Joy's a mom, and she knows about mops. And here she is with her new Miracle Mop. Joy, take it away."

And then I froze.

I just completely froze.

Being on live TV was never, ever my goal.

I never dreamed about it, or expected it, or thought it could ever happen. My goal was to get my mops into hardware stores and Kmarts and other retail outlets. I mean, just months earlier I hadn't even known QVC existed.

So what did it mean that I was suddenly standing on a rotating stage in front of millions of people, live on the air?

If you think about it in the traditional sense, it meant that I had failed.

I had a plan to become successful, and I didn't stick to that plan. I was on an entirely new and different path from the one I should have been staying on. If the plan was to go from A to Z, I took a detour that wasn't even in the same alphabet! I got to B or C or D and made a hard right turn to who knows where.

You'll hear lots of people say things like *Don't take your eyes off the prize* and *Stay focused on your ultimate goal.* Well, by those standards, I blew it.

I didn't stick to the plan.

But staying focused on the finish line would *not* have been good advice for me in that moment. The only thing that mattered, at that very moment, was that I take the single next step I needed to take.

So I took my eyes off the finish line, and I did what I needed to do to keep moving forward.

The host's introductory words stuck in my head—they sounded kind of sarcastic. *Oh, here's a mom and her mop.* But that's not what made me freeze. I froze because I realized we were live. I was being beamed into 90 million homes—*90 million!* Standing in front of a big chunk of America, holding a mop! How did this happen? How did I get here? Was this even real?

Yes, it was real. It was happening. It was happening *now.* And in an instant my mind unfroze and I focused on one thing and one thing only—the single precise step I had to take next.

Talk.

*Just start talking, Joy. That's all you have to do.*

And so I did. With the lights nearly blinding me and millions of people watching me and my heart still beating wildly, I started talking.

"You know what it's like to have to bend down and wring out a mop, don't you?" I said. "It's hard work. I know, I do it all the time. Well, let me show you this."

And then I showed America the Miracle Mop.

I covered everything. I mopped up a spill with ease and wrung out the mop into a bucket just as easily. I talked about the detachable head and how it was made with 300 feet of continuous-loop cotton, and how absorbent the cotton was and how simple it was to use, and how it would make our lives a little easier, a little better, each and every day. The words were just there. They just came out. It felt natural and right. It felt just like when I talked about the mop to one curious mom at a boat show.

In the background, I heard the faint sound of a telephone ringing.

"Let's go to a call," I heard the host say.

"Hi, Joy," I heard the caller's piped-in voice say.

"Well, hello, how are you?" I said back.

"You know, Joy, I have a really bad back, and this is just what I need. This mop sounds amazing."

More telephones rang. I kept talking. Off to the side, out of camera range, there was a monitor that counted the number of orders coming in and the number of Miracle Mops sold. Early on, I glanced at it and saw that 50 mops had been sold. The next time I glanced at it, it was 100. Then 200. The phones kept ringing, and I kept talking. Kept talking, kept mopping, kept wringing. Kept moving forward. The segment was supposed to run for fifteen minutes.

But they ended it early. Again.

The cameras turned off and technicians scrambled about, and at first I wasn't sure what had happened. It all went by so quickly, in a blur. Then I saw Dan coming toward me.

With a really big grin.

"You broke the phones," he said.

"I did what?"

The off-camera monitor showed the volume of calls. A green line represented people ordering the mops. A darker green line was for people waiting on hold to order the mops. But the line wasn't green. It wasn't dark green.

It was pink.

And pink meant the system was overloaded.

"Joy, we sold out," Dan went on.

"What?" I said, wanting to hear him say it again.

"You sold all the mops, Joy. You sold them all."

In just twelve minutes, we'd sold 4,500 Miracle Mops.

There wasn't a single mop left to return to vendor.

# 27

Everything happened so quickly after that.

Almost immediately, Dan placed another order. This time, he wanted us to bring 18,000 Miracle Mops with us. *Eighteen thousand mops!*

I went to the auto body shop and huddled with my father. Rudy kept handling the money side of things, while I concentrated on selling the mops. I knew the auto body shop was doing really good business, and it never seemed to be a problem for Rudy to come up with more money for more mops.

"Don't worry about it," he told me again. "I'll take care of it."

We had West Coast manufacture 18,000 Miracle Mops, and I went back on the air at QVC.

In twenty minutes, we sold all 18,000 Miracle Mops.

Then Dan placed another order.

This time, he wanted 60,000 mops.

*Sixty thousand mops!*

Hearing that number made me feel two things—exhilaration and panic. Those two feelings were coming hand in hand a lot lately.

The problem with making so many mops was cash flow. There was a huge time lag between when we had to spend money to make more mops and when we got paid for those mops once they sold on QVC. I'm sure bigger companies could handle that kind of problem, but I wasn't a big company. I was just little old me.

I called Dan and asked him for a partial advance on sales. That was not the way QVC operated—ever—and I knew it. But I felt I had a special product, and I knew Dan believed in it, too.

"We went from zero to sixty so fast, Dan," I told him. "I don't have the money to make 60,000 mops. Can we do a partial prepayment?"

Dan said yes. He had the instincts and vision to see the potential of my mop, and he also believed in me. We were in business again. Rudy contacted West Coast and put in the order for 60,000 mops.

But there was a problem.

"Joy, bad news," Rudy told me. "They're raising the price by almost two dollars a mop."

I was stunned. I was floored. I never saw that coming. We had a deal with West Coast to make the mops at a cost that allowed QVC to charge $19.99 for each one. If West Coast raised the cost we had negotiated by two dollars, we wouldn't be able to sell the mops at that price and make any money. I knew right away what was happening.

It was a shakedown.

But that wasn't even the worst of it.

It was obvious to me that the men who were manufacturing the mops at West Coast saw how successful we had been on QVC. All of a sudden, they realized they were sitting on something that could be worth millions of dollars. They had the molds, and they had the factory.

What did they need me for?

To them, I was just Rudy's daughter. They must have figured that by raising the cost that much, they could push us out of the process.

They were trying to steal my mop.

But there was a solution.

I could talk to Eddie Arnolds, the man who represented the Australian company that held the patent—and the man who had connected us to West Coast in the first place—and I could have him make West Coast give us back the molds so I could find a new manufacturer to make the 60,000 mops.

I told my father to call Eddie and tell West Coast we wanted our molds back.

"We can't do that, Joy," my father said.

"Why not?"

"Eddie's not going to get us the molds because we owe them money."

"We owe who money? What are you talking about?"

I felt a terrible, sinking feeling. I'd been okay with my father handling the financial side of things, even though I hadn't made any money yet from our sales. I assumed it was all being put back into the business. But now it was dawning on me that I'd been naive. I should have paid more attention. For the first time, I started to ask Rudy questions about our finances.

"Who do we owe?" I asked.

"Eddie."

"Eddie? How much?"

"Hundreds of thousands."

"For what?!"

"Well . . ."

It turned out Rudy had never directly paid West Coast for the molds or for anything. He always sent money to Eddie, and Eddie paid West Coast. Then Rudy stopped paying Eddie altogether.

"Why did you stop?" I demanded.

"Well . . ."

There were no good answers. The whole thing was a mess. Then I got another shock. Most of the money for the mops hadn't come from the auto body shop, as I thought it had.

It came from Rudy's girlfriend, Thelma.

Which meant that Thelma was making the decisions.

We sat down and had a meeting at the shop—Rudy and Thelma and me. I explained that I had to get the molds back one way or another. Every dollar I'd made from selling the mops—through Amway, through Kmart, through QVC—had gone straight back into the business. There was too much at stake for me to just walk away because West Coast raised the price. We had to find some way to get back control of the Miracle Mop.

But Thelma didn't want to hear it.

"Joy, we can't pay those bills—we don't have the money," she said. "That's it, it's a done deal. It's all over."

"No, no, no, wait a minute . . ."

"Joy, she's right," Rudy said. "We don't have the money. It's over. That's it. We're through."

Another terrible realization hit me. West Coast had the molds and the money and the capacity to make the 60,000 mops, and their partner Eddie had the patent. We had nothing but my father's sloppy paperwork and a mountain of debt.

They weren't trying to steal the Miracle Mop away from me.

*They'd already stolen it.*

"Give me all the books," I told Rudy. "Every bill, every receipt, everything. I'm going to figure this out."

That night, I took a box filled with folders and papers home with me. I dropped it on the kitchen table with a thud and spent the next few hours reading through it all.

Somewhere in that box, I had to believe, was the answer. It *had* to be there. It had to had to had to had to had to be there.

And then the most remarkable thing happened.

# 28

In the box of papers, I found the patent from the Australian company that Eddie originally sent us when he mailed us that first metal mop.

I hadn't really looked over the patent too carefully before, but now I did. It was technical, with drawings and numbers and functional terms, but I understood enough of it. I looked at it for an hour, and then another hour. I studied every letter and number and line. Something about it didn't seem right to me. Finally, I realized what it was.

It was so simple, I couldn't believe we had missed it.

The patent in my hand was *not* for the metal mop the company sent us.

The patent was for a different mop that had nothing to do with the self-wringing concept I'd come up with!

Because Eddie sent us the patent at the same time he sent us the metal mop, Rudy and his lawyer had assumed the patent was for that mop. But it wasn't. I didn't need Eddie's patent to make the Miracle Mop because he didn't have the patent for my idea. I had never needed Eddie in the first place. The whole deal we made with him was a fraud!

I got up from the kitchen table and ran around the house waving the patent in the air and screaming. I'm sure I woke up the children.

Then I called Ronni.

"Those liars!" I yelled into the phone. "How could they do this?"

I don't think I've ever been angrier in my life. I was seeing red. These people were cheats and liars, and they were trying to steal my idea. They were playing games with my future—with my *children's* future.

They must have assumed some lowly single mom from Long Island wouldn't be able to stop them.

They were wrong.

I sat down and came up with a plan.

The biggest problem was that, because of the way my father had worked out the deal with Eddie, there was no trace of us owning any part of the molds.

All the money he sent went straight to Eddie, who then sent it to West Coast Molds & Manufacturing. All the important paperwork about the molds was between Eddie and West Coast, and Rudy had no receipts for the mold payments we had made.

From the outside looking in, there was no legal proof that we had paid for, or owned, the molds.

So I had to find a way to get Eddie to cancel the deal, give up his role in making the Miracle Mop, and sign something that confirmed we owned the molds.

But how?

From the start, I had a suspicion that Eddie might not be the most reputable businessman in the world. Then I thought—if he could be so heartless with a single mom from Long Island, who else might he have tried to swindle along the way?

I did more research, and I learned that in addition to handling the mop patent for the Australian company, Eddie also sold a good number of books published by them. What if there was something shady about that deal, too? I decided I needed to call the company's owner and, without setting off any alarm bells, get more information.

I found the owner's phone number and called him in the middle of the night my time, which was the middle of the day halfway around the world. The owner was friendly and pleasant. I told him who I was, and, after talking a little bit about the mop business, I asked him if Eddie had been sending him royalties for the sales of the Miracle Mop.

"No, he hasn't yet," the owner said.

I was shocked. We'd had lots of sales by then. How could he not have received any royalties from Eddie? There had to be something fishy going on. Then I casually asked him about royalties from the book sales, to get a sense of whether Eddie had been holding them back, too.

He said he hadn't received those, either.

The owner didn't suspect anything was wrong, but I knew. From my research, I knew that Eddie was selling a whole lot of books. Which meant I was right. Eddie was cheating his boss in Australia, too.

That was the leverage I needed. I called Eddie in Texas, where he was living, and told him I wanted a face-to-face meeting. He said no.

"It's in your best interest to see me," I said.

He finally agreed to meet me in a hotel room in Texas. I called Tony and asked him if he could come over and watch the children for a couple of days, and I booked a flight to Texas for Ronni and me. But there was another problem.

Ronni *hated* to fly.

In fact, she hadn't been on an airplane in *ten years*.

"You have to suck it up," I told her. "We just have to do this."

When I met Ronni at the airport, she seemed strangely calm. She explained she'd taken some relaxants and had a glass or two of wine—even though it was nine in the morning. It was the only way she could fly, she explained. Once we were on the plane, though, her fear of flying got the best of her anyway.

"Did they shut the door yet?" she asked me, her voice rising higher and higher. "Tell me if they shut it yet. No, wait, don't tell me. I don't want to know. Okay, tell me. Did they shut it yet? I need to know if they shut it yet. I need to know. No wait, don't tell me. Okay, tell me."

When an attendant finally did shut the plane door, Ronni freaked out. She started jabbering uncontrollably to the person sitting next to her. Somehow she made it through the flight, and the unlucky passenger next to her did, too.

We landed in Texas and got ready to meet Eddie.

Ronni and I got to the hotel room first. I'd been meeting with a new lawyer in New York, John Calcagni, to prepare my case, and I had a stack of legal documents that I spread out on the small table in the hotel room. This was the proof that Eddie was cheating his boss in Australia, and that he was cheating us, too.

Before Eddie arrived, I sat on the bed and tried to calm myself down. I knew that I was in the right, and Eddie was in the wrong. I knew that without any doubt at all. What I didn't know was how Eddie would react. Would he be able to explain it all? Would he even care? Would he try to intimidate me? It was like a big chess game, except with very real stakes.

Eddie was late, but finally we heard a knock on the door. My heart jumped. I opened the door, and Eddie stood there wearing a silk designer suit and expensive shoes. He seemed so confident, so sure of himself. Like he already knew what the outcome of the meeting would be. I motioned for him to come in.

Then I got right to it.

"I know what you did," I said as soon as Eddie sat down at the table. "I know what you're trying to do to me and my three children. When you leave this room, you're either going to agree to everything I say, or you will be sued a hundred different ways."

Eddie looked at me and smiled. Like he didn't have a care in the world.

"Who the hell do you think you are?" he said.

There are some people in the business world who think it's okay to treat people poorly. "It's just business," you'll hear them say. A lawyer or an entrepreneur who is trying to get an edge acts in a shady way in their dealings—but that's okay, they believe, so long as they're upstanding citizens at home. They think it's okay to lie in their office, but not in their living room.

I disagree.

For me, there isn't any difference between business and life. There isn't one "business" Joy and one "mom" Joy. There is only Joy. I operate under the same governing principles in all aspects of my life—I want to be a strong, kind, decent person who is forceful but fair. I can't work any other way.

I don't think we can say, "Oh, this isn't who I am, this is just business."

I believe that what we do *is* who we are.

How can we say that what we do at work doesn't define who we are? How can something we do for eight to twelve hours a day *not* define who we are? No matter what work we do—politician, policeman, construction worker, ice cream salesman—the hours we spend working reflect our unique and special gifts as human beings. They reflect who we are and how we conduct ourselves in the world.

I believe my business and my life are interconnected, and I need my personal morality to infuse everything I do in *all* walks of life.

Because as long as we have goodness and decency and morality on our side—and as long as we understand that what we do *is* who we are— we will have the strength and the power to accomplish *anything*.

Eddie was trying to scare me. He was testing me to see how tough I was. Out of the corner of my eye, I saw Ronni sitting on the bed, her leg shaking and bouncing all over the place, because that's what she does when she gets nervous. Believe me, I was nervous, too.

But I didn't let Eddie see that, and I didn't let up. I showed him all the paperwork. I told him I knew he'd committed fraud. I told him I knew he'd cheated his Australian boss out of book royalties, too, even though I had no idea to what degree.

"No, no, no, you have it all wrong," Eddie kept saying.

But I kept pushing. I was practically thundering! And the harder I pushed, the more Eddie began to squirm. And that emboldened me. I went at him even harder. Honestly, it was like I was in someone else's body. I was *lethal*. I stood over Eddie and berated him and shook my finger at him and gave him everything I had.

"If you don't do what I want you to do, I will call your boss in Australia, and he will look into every transaction he made with you for the last ten years!" I huffed. "You tried to destroy me? You tried to destroy my three children? That is *not* going to happen."

Seriously, who was I? Who was saying all these things? This wasn't some gangster movie, this was real life! But I was in a zone, and I meant what I was saying, every word of it. I was in the right, and I had all the power in the world.

Bit by bit, I started to see the fight go out of Eddie. I could literally see him sag in his chair. I put three sheets of paper in front of him, and I put a pen next to the papers.

"These are what you need to sign," I said.

One of the documents established that Eddie would no longer receive royalties of any kind from the Miracle Mop. The second one explained that the molds for the mop were owned by me and not by him or West Coast Molds & Manufacturing. And the third one made clear that we didn't owe Eddie a single penny. We were cutting him loose. We were getting him out of our lives.

"You need to sign these papers," I said. "You have no choice."

Eddie picked up the pen and signed all three papers.

Then he got up from the table, straightened his tie, and walked to the door. Just before he left, he turned and said two parting words to me. The first one is unprintable.

The second one was "you."

# 29

When the door closed behind Eddie, I realized that my hands were trembling. If I'd had a cigarette, I wouldn't have been able to light it. Ronni was shaking, too.

But—I had paperwork that proved I owned the molds! All I had to do was go to California and get them.

Back in New York, I had another meeting with my lawyer, John Calcagni, and he connected me to a lawyer in California, Keith Gregory. John and Keith helped me make sure I was doing everything right. We set up a meeting with West Coast Molds & Manufacturing, and the plan was to pay them what Rudy owed them and come back home with our molds.

But first, I had another meeting with Rudy and Thelma.

As far as they were concerned, the Miracle Mop was dead. They were ready to write the whole thing off. All they saw was money going out, and they didn't want to put another nickel into the business. They'd already accepted that much of what they'd invested was lost.

But I had a deal for them.

I promised Thelma that if she put up the money to pay West Coast what we owed them, I would pay her back everything she and Rudy had put into the business. Not some of it—*all* of it. Every last penny, plus interest. I didn't care how long it took, but I would see to it that they didn't lose a single dollar because of the Miracle Mop. There was only one condition.

"From now on," I told them, "neither of you will have anything to do with the Miracle Mop. The business will be mine—all of it."

It was a good deal for them. They'd already accepted losing a really big chunk of money. Now they had some hope of getting it back.

Thelma gave me the funds to pay back West Coast.

I brought my children with me to California, along with Suzy, a neighbor who sometimes babysat for them. This was just another one of our family adventures. Our New York lawyer, John, came out with us, too, and so did Ronni. Suzy watched the children in our hotel room while Ronni and I rented a car and drove to the West Coast facility in Irvine, about an hour south of Los Angeles.

When we got there, I told the receptionist, "We need to speak with Bill."

The first time I met Bill, back when we started working with West Coast, he was incredibly friendly. He even invited me to his home to meet his family. This time, though, when we walked into his office, he barely made eye contact. He was all business, or all something.

He was sitting at his desk with an open can of Pepsi in front of him.

I took the seat across from his desk. I took out the cashier's check for the money Rudy hadn't paid West Coast, and put it on the desk, facing him. Bill looked at it, but he didn't touch it. I told him all I needed were the molds.

"We don't have the molds," Bill said calmly.

"What? What are you talking about?"

"They were stolen," he said.

I was astonished. Absolutely floored. Not because I believed him, which I didn't, but because he was so calm while he was lying to my face. It was as if he was saying, *You stupid little girl, you're not going to push me around like you did Eddie.* I felt so much anger and frustration that I could barely stand it. First Eddie, and now this? The molds were gone? Stolen? Are you kidding me???

"Tell you what," Bill said. "We'll have another look around and see if we can't find them. We'll call you if we do."

That was it. I'd had enough.

I jumped up from my chair, and I grabbed Bill's can of Pepsi, and I picked it up and I slammed it down on his desk *so hard* that the can crumpled and the soda shot out everywhere. All over the desk, all over his suit, all over everything. Bill just looked at me with a stunned expression, drops of Pepsi dripping down his face.

"You're not going to get away with this," I said.

Then I stormed out of his office.

Ronni and I got into the rental car and drove around the parking lot, looking for the truck where they might be hiding our molds. I don't know whose idea it was; probably it was mine.

"Joy, what if we find the truck?" Ronni asked. "What do we do then?"

"I don't know, Ronni."

"What if they have a gun? I might be crazy, but I'm not stupid."

After a few minutes we gave up and drove back to the hotel. I got dinner for the children and tried to settle myself down. After dinner, I did my best to tuck the children into bed, but they were too excited to sleep, so I let them watch TV. Then I got into the rental car and drove to Keith's law office. It was pretty late by then. John Calcagni was there, too, and I told him everything that had happened. I was still livid, still boiling. But also scared at the same time.

"Okay, so what now?" I said. "We take Bill to court and we get him to give up the molds, right?"

"It doesn't work that way," Keith said. "The very best you can expect to get out of the judge is a promise to look into it."

"Look into it? How long will that take?"

Keith hesitated.

"Months," he finally said.

"Oh, no, no, no," I said, my voice rising. "I can't do that. I can't wait months. We have to get the mops to QVC. Can't we get the judge to issue some kind of emergency order?"

"That's called a conversion, and I've never seen it happen," Keith said. "And it's not the right way to go. If the judge says no to the emergency conversion, I will have to appeal it, and that will add even more months to it. It will make everything harder."

I looked at John, and he said he agreed with Keith.

"But the proof!" I said. "We have the proof right here! You have to find a way!"

I was trying to push them into my mind-set, where getting the molds back in a day *was* possible, and all we had to do was figure out how. But it wasn't easy. They knew how things worked, and they knew my chances of getting the molds back that quickly were all but zero.

"Okay, let's talk it over," Keith finally said. "But Joy, you need to understand that this is the biggest long shot. No judge is going to make a decision in one day. And then you'll be stuck."

"I don't care," I said. "I have no choice. I have to get those molds. Now, how are we going to do it?"

We stayed in Keith's office until 2:00 a.m., trying to figure it out.

# 30

Early the next morning, I set out for a courtroom in Irvine for the emergency hearing.

The judge was an older, distinguished man with gray hair. Bill from West Coast and his attorney, and several other men in expensive suits, sat at one table in front of the judge. Keith and John and I sat at the other. For the first half hour of the hearing, the lawyers argued back and forth about who was right and who was wrong.

"She has the signed documents," Keith said. "She has the cashier's check. She has the entire history of this transaction."

"Your Honor, you cannot make a decision on the spot," their lawyer interrupted. "This is our business. We made these molds in good faith."

It was right around then that I started tugging on Keith's sleeve.

Keith knew what that meant. The night before, I'd asked him if I could address the judge directly. He said we would see how it went. But I didn't want to wait any longer. I wanted to talk to the judge myself.

"Your Honor, may Joy address the court?" Keith finally asked.

The judge nodded yes. I got up from my chair.

A familiar feeling bubbled up—the same feeling I had had when I was on the rotating stage at QVC.

*Everything is at stake. Right here, right now. This very moment.*

"Your Honor," I said, "I know what we are asking for today is unusual. But I need you to understand what I'm fighting for. This isn't a business to me. This is my life."

And I went on. I told the judge everything. The whole story. About my marriage and my divorce and my three children. About creating the mop and paying for the molds. About going on QVC and selling them myself. About putting all my savings into the business. West Coast's lawyer objected two or three times, but the judge let me keep going.

"Your Honor, if I don't go back home with these molds, everything I have worked on my whole life will be lost. Everything, all of it, gone. I have tried to do everything right. I've been on the right side with every step, and they've been on the wrong side. Your Honor, I hope you can make a decision for what is right."

The courtroom fell silent. The judge picked up his glasses and asked to see some documents again. I held my breath. Keith patted me on the arm to try to assure me.

It struck me as the kind of pat you give to someone who lost.

"I've made my decision," the judge finally said.

I felt like I might be sick.

There was no legal precedent for a decision in my favor. The odds were stacked against me. My own lawyers didn't believe I could do anything to make a difference. But I spoke up anyway. I spoke up for myself. Why?

Because my voice mattered.

That's the thing—all of our voices matter, and all of us can make a difference, even when the odds are stacked against us. And the way we can make a difference is by speaking up for ourselves.

When the boys in the playground were picking on my cousin Phil and I rushed in to confront them, it was one skinny girl against a whole pack of boys—but I didn't let that stop me. I spoke up for myself, and I spoke up for Phil. I made my voice heard. And it made a difference.

When I stood up to my father after he smashed my chocolate snaps, that made a difference, too. When I spoke up for myself to the buyer from Kmart, and to Dan at QVC, and to Eddie in the hotel room, speaking up made a huge difference. In fact, it made *all* the difference.

We cannot be afraid to speak up for ourselves, because we are the best ones to speak up for us. We are our best advocates, our best champions. When we make our voices heard, we empower ourselves in a way that few other things can.

Believe me, I was scared to get up in front of the judge and tell him my whole life story. But I did it anyway, because I had no choice.

And besides, there wasn't anyone better in the world to speak up for me than me.

So while it might have been a legal long shot, I knew I was in the right. I knew that what I was fighting for was fair. If we're on the side of good, we can never be afraid to speak up. And we must believe that speaking up for ourselves can make all the difference in the world.

The judge looked straight at me as he issued his decision. It was as if he was talking directly to me.

"I am ordering an emergency conversion of goods for noon tomorrow," he said in a deep voice. "At that time, the sheriffs are going to this address, and they are going to supervise the collection of these molds, and they are going to watch as they are all handed over to Joy."

But there was more, and this time the judge faced the team from West Coast.

"Once the molds are in her possession, she will hand over the bank check for what is owed to West Coast Molds & Manufacturing," the judge continued. "If you do not produce the molds and deliver them to the petitioner, the sheriffs at the scene have the full authority to place you under arrest."

Then the judge looked at me again.

"I assume you will be there tomorrow at noon?" he asked.

"Yes, Your Honor, I will be there," I said.

The judge banged down his gavel.

"Court is adjourned."

# 31

I looked at Keith, and he looked at me. Then we both broke out in big smiles.

Keith was flabbergasted. He couldn't believe what we'd just heard. Much later, he would write an article for a law journal about my case. It was about how a single mom from Long Island overcame staggering odds and got her mop molds back—and, in the process, made legal history.

The next day was like something out of a movie. I hired two drivers to show up with a truck at the West Coast facility. Bill was there, and he didn't look pleased. A West Coast truck pulled up, and one by one the mop molds were moved from their truck to ours. A sheriff stood right next to me, watching every move. When the molds were all packed up, I gave the truck drivers the $1,000 I promised them for driving the molds cross-country to Long Island.

"If you don't stop except to eat and go to the bathroom, I'll give you another $1,000 when you get there," I told them. My mop molds had been kidnapped before. I wasn't going to let anything else to happen to them.

It was only then, once the molds were on their way across the country, that the reality of what had happened sank in.

Yes, I had the molds back.

But now I had to make 60,000 Miracle Mops.

And so far, I'd never made even *one*.

What had I gotten myself into?

I was still in California when I called Richie, the manager of my father's auto body shop. Richie was the guy who gave me such a hard time about the naked photos I took off the back room walls.

"I need to make 60,000 mops in six months," I said. "Can you help me?"

Richie didn't hesitate.

"You bet," he said.

I flew back to New York and went straight to our little office in the auto body shop. Somehow, I had to assemble an entire manufacturing operation, and I had to do it really quickly. I didn't know where to begin, so I ran my hands across my office desk to get rid of the dust. Cleaning seemed to be as good a place to start as any. Then I walked into the bathroom to wash my hands.

I opened the bathroom door, and immediately I noticed something had changed.

Richie had taken down the last of the naked women photos.

It was a gesture. A message to me.

*Joy, we've got your back.*

# 32

On the flight back home from California, in between rounds of trying to keep Ronni calm, I did some math in my head.

Somehow, I had to create, test, package, and ship 60,000 mops in six months. Even for West Coast, which had manufacturing machines and experienced workers, turning out that many mops in just a few months' time would have been a challenge.

But I had none of that. No machines, no seasoned employees. No employees *period*. I didn't even have the raw supplies I needed to make the mops.

But okay—even if I somehow found a way to manufacture the mops, and even if I was somehow able to assemble ten mops every hour for twenty-four hours a day, seven days a week, at the end of six months I'd have 43,200 mops.

That would be a full-blown miracle—but we'd still be short more than 16,000 mops.

So what was I supposed to do?

Sitting on the plane, I looked over at my children—Christie, Bobby, and Jackie. They were sleeping, and they looked so small in their seats. I stared at their little faces for a long time, and it made me feel better. My children *always* made me feel better.

But more than that, my children made me feel like I could accomplish anything. Because, after all, I didn't have a choice. I had to find a way to make those mops for them.

So while I may not have had any machines or employees or raw materials, I did have one thing going for me, and it was my secret weapon.

I had my family.

All the drama and excitement with the Miracle Mop happened at the same time the children and I were adjusting to life without Tony.

My youngest, Jackie, was so young when Tony left, and she doesn't really remember all of us being together. Bobby, who was two years older, was a little more aware of what was happening.

But Christie was in kindergarten when Tony and I split up, and she had the most to deal with. She was the oldest, and she saw and absorbed more than the other kids. She saw a lot of the fighting, and she saw how painful the divorce was for me. I felt such a sadness that someone so young had to shoulder the heartbreak of a family coming apart.

Christie had more questions for me than the other kids, and I tried to be honest and open about everything, without burdening her too much. The main thing I needed her to know was that Tony was not a bad man.

He was who he was, and I was who I was. We loved each other, but we simply couldn't find a way to stay married to each other. Christie was smart enough to grasp that, even at her young age.

When I look back now, though, I know that Christie may have been forced to grow up a little more quickly than she should have. When the breakup happened, and then everything with the Miracle Mop, Christie's instinct was to do whatever she could to make things easier for me. Can you imagine that? Someone so young deciding it's her responsibility to lessen her mother's burden? It makes me want to cry just thinking about it. But that's what Christie instinctively felt—that I couldn't possibly do everything all by myself, and that it was her job to help me as much as she could, on all levels.

I was lucky. Really lucky. All my children were amazing.

Very early on, I made an important decision. It was one of the best decisions I ever made, and it has shaped my life to its core, even today.

I decided that, no matter what, my children and I would always be a team.

Through good and bad—through anything—the four of us would remain a tight, inseparable unit. The Core Four, as Jackie later called us. And to do that, I had to treat the children as adults whenever I could.

That's why I always took my children with me on business trips.

I took them with me to Kmart for my Miracle Mop demonstrations, and they remember playing in the aisles and snacking on the food from all the kitchen demos.

I took them with me to the QVC segments, and they remember flying kites with Ronni and me in the back of the hotel.

I took them with me to California to see about the molds, and they remember us joining in on the Easter egg hunt at our hotel.

A lot of their childhood memories are of things that sprang out of creating and selling the Miracle Mop. And that was by design.

I decided that as long as I was going to be busy chasing my dream, I wanted my kids to be chasing it with me. I wanted them to be a part of it. I wanted all of us to do it *together*. Like I said, there wasn't one "business" Joy and one "mom" Joy. There was just Joy. And everything I said or did came from the same place.

It came from my heart.

For a long time after Tony left, my children and I all slept in the same room. I think it started because a very young Jackie had this thing where she never wanted to be the last person out of the four of us to fall asleep. So she came to sleep with me in my bed, because she knew I'd always outlast her.

Then Bobby came in and started curling up in a sleeping bag on the floor at the foot of my bed. Then Christie, not wanting to be left out, did the same thing at the side of my bed. And that's how we slept, the four of us huddled in and around my bed, for many years.

And I would lie there, in my bed, reliving all the drama and stress of the day, adding up numbers, making decisions and unmaking them, trying to clear my head but being unable to, until finally I'd put on my headphones and blast Celine Dion in my Discman at nearly full volume as a way to block out the day.

And Christie would hum along to the songs because I played them so loud that she could hear them through the headphones. And Bobby would pop up to say hello every now and then before finally falling asleep. And Jackie would snuggle up against me until she, too, slipped away to dreamland.

And that's how I would fall asleep every night, surrounded by my children, from start to finish, the Core Four, forever.

The delivery truck with the mop molds made it safely back to Long Island. I can't tell you how relieved I was to finally have the molds in front of me at my father's shop.

Richie and the other mechanics had been witness to the creation of the Miracle Mop over the years, so when I asked them for their help, they were already familiar with the process. They were hard workers, and really skilled, and having them on board was a huge positive. They were the first people I ever hired.

Then there was my father. I'd taken control of the company and I had no doubt I'd done the right thing. But that didn't mean my father couldn't be a part of what I was doing. After all, he was a part of my life in a lot of ways, and he even babysat the children for me when I needed him to. I asked Rudy if we could run the Miracle Mop operation out of his auto body shop, and take over all four of the bays behind the shop and use them for manufacturing space. He agreed. It was a business arrangement, but it was more than that.

It was my father being there for me when I needed him.

So now I had a makeshift manufacturing facility. And I had the advance money from QVC, which I used to order the parts and supplies that we needed. One of the first things I did was buy four big commercial sewing machines, and a commercial loom, to process the many thousands of yards of cotton yarn I ordered for the mop heads.

But the standard loom wasn't ideal for looping our dense, single-strand cotton into the shape of a mop head, so Richie and the guys looked at the special loom West Coast used, and created an even better one for us.

Then I ordered the mop poles, which I learned had to come from the only company in the country that could meet our specifications. The poles had to be substantial enough to support a hook on the inside, but pliant enough to adhere to the glue that fused all the plastic parts together. The inner and outer diameters had to be just right. Plus, they couldn't be made of wood, because wood rots. And they couldn't be made of metal, because metal rusts. They had to be made of the same strong plastic they use to make car bumpers.

Only one company had the sophistication to produce such a pole, and it was a California company that specialized in irrigation piping.

Our mop handle, I learned, was basically a sprinkler pipe.

I placed a huge order with the company, and the pipes were hauled across the country on flatbed trucks. Each pipe was twenty-five feet long when it arrived, so we had to cut them down to mop-size in the shop.

Our biggest problem, I knew all along, was going to be people. Where was I going to find the workers to put the mops together?

Even with Richie and the other guys, and me and Rudy and Ronni, and even Christie and Bobby and Jackie pitching in, we'd be painfully understaffed. I couldn't go through a big hiring process, because we needed to start right away. Richie and I had already begun gluing the mop handles together, and he'd brought in his twenty-year-old daughter to help. But it was tricky work, and it wasn't going well. And with each hour that passed, we just fell further and further behind.

Luckily, I had an idea.

# 33

A few months earlier, a pastor had knocked on the door of Rudy's shop. The pastor said that he ran a church in nearby Deer Park, and his congregation included a number of Spanish-speaking immigrants who were looking for jobs. The pastor was going from business to business, knocking on doors, seeing if anyone was hiring. I thanked him and told him I didn't need any workers at the time.

But now, I did.

I got in the old Lumina and drove all over Deer Park, looking for the church. I'd forgotten its name, so I had to try a few before I found it. The pastor was standing out in front, as if he'd been waiting for me.

"I need women who can sew and men who can machine," I told him. "I need hardworking people who can work crazy hours. It's good pay, but it's hard work. Can you help?"

The pastor just smiled.

Later that day, he was back at the auto body shop with about twenty men and women standing behind him.

They were from El Salvador and other neighboring countries, and they spoke only Spanish. I looked at their faces, and they seemed as apprehensive as I did. They didn't know what they were getting into, and neither did I. With the pastor translating for me, I explained the process of looming and sewing the mop heads.

"I need you to sew these mop heads together perfectly, and I need you to sew a *lot* of them," I said. I left out the part about needing 60,000. It didn't seem like the best time to share that information.

Some of the women sat down at the sewing machines, and some others at the loom. Richie took the men to the mop assembly table. We went through all the steps together. Explaining it was complicated, and at first the women at the sewing machines seemed, I don't know, disengaged. I wasn't sure if they were getting it, and I had a moment of panic. I felt lucky to have found them, but if they didn't work out, I had no Plan B. This was it. This *had* to work out.

Then I stepped back, and the women got to work. I held my breath as I watched them move the cotton strands through the loom and the sewing machines. What happened next was a shock.

Within a couple of minutes, they were flying.

Their hands were a blur. They knew how to do it. Heck, they knew how to do it a lot better than we'd been doing it!

And when I saw them working with such speed and skill and authority, a wave of euphoria washed over me. I mean, I was *ecstatic*.

I literally ran around the shop kissing every one of the women on the cheek. Then I ran around and kissed them again! Tears were streaming down my cheeks! They must have thought I was crazy.

But I wasn't crazy. I was just so grateful.

These women were my saviors.

The next few months were sheer madness.

The slowest part of the process was looming the mop heads, and the men I hired were making new looms as fast as they could. But it still wasn't happening fast enough. We needed more workers, so I asked the women if they had any brothers, cousins, friends, whatever, who needed work. Eventually, we had enough people to set up three shifts of different workers so we could keep making the mops around the clock.

Even my children were helping out. Most days, when they weren't in school, they were in the shop with us, doing whatever they could to pitch in. One of the problems with my design for the continuous-loop mop head was that, as you looped the cotton around and around and around the loom, you had to keep the strands together in the right shape so you could carry them over to the sewing machines. Our solution for that was using plain old drinking straws and sticking them in between the strands. It wasn't rocket science, but the straws held the shape.

But when the straws I ordered finally arrived, I discovered each one was individually wrapped in paper. Oh, Lord. So now we had to unwrap each and every one before we could use it.

That became Bobby's and Jackie's job. They came to the shop and unwrapped hundreds and hundreds of straws. And they made it fun. Lots of wrappers and spitballs flying everywhere.

Meanwhile, Christie worked on sealing the bags the mops would be shipped in, even though for part of the time she had a cast on her arm after jumping out of her friend's treehouse.

The shop was never quiet. It was always humming with activity. We had the radio on constantly, and when we got hungry we ordered lots of pizzas and hamburgers and Chinese food. There were times when—for me at least—it all felt like one big party.

But the truth is, everyone was working *incredibly* hard. We put in long, long hours, night after night, week after week. Many nights, I'd have to approach one of our seamstresses and ask her if she could stay a few more hours, until 1:00 a.m. or even later. I knew they had children at home, just like I did, so it was difficult to ask. But they always said yes. They leaned on their families, and they always found a way to stay.

Everyone bought into what we were doing. They understood they were part of something special, and they were incredibly devoted. Their work ethic was unlike anything I'd ever seen before. Every morning they walked to the shop, or rode their bicycles there, or hitched rides with friends, and every day they worked nearly nonstop, quickly and efficiently. Finding them was one of the happiest accidents of my life.

And *still*, it was touch and go. The weeks and months would pass and it seemed like we never got any closer to actually finishing the job. There were *always* more mops to make.

With just a week to go before the mops were due at QVC, we still had several thousand mops to complete.

The last few days all blended together into one long, unending, frantic blur. On the morning of the actual due date, when the delivery trucks pulled into the back bays to pick up the last of the mops, we *still* weren't done. So the truck drivers waited while we kept working.

And then—we did it. We made the 60,000th Miracle Mop.

We made it with negative zero minutes to spare.

I stood out on the back bays, along with Richie and Ronni and the mechanics and the men and women from the church and my children, watching as the drivers loaded the last pallet of mops into a truck. When the driver packed in the last pallet and pulled the back hatch shut, we all let out a howling cheer. We laughed and hugged and whooped it up. It was one of the sweetest, most heartfelt celebrations of my life.

I didn't know whether to laugh or cry or scream or all three.

We did it. We made 60,000 perfect mops. This ragtag group, each of us there for different reasons—we worked together as a team and we did it.

The name of the mop was never more appropriate, because what we did was a miracle.

You will always hear the same warning about working with your loved ones—never mix business with family, because it can get messy.

Well, the messy part is true.

But I think you should lean on your family anyway.

I wouldn't have been able to make 60,000 Miracle Mops if it hadn't been for my family. I needed my father Rudy to be involved and I needed every bit of help and support I got from my children.

But the women from the church also had to rely on *their* families. When they worked late, a mother or a father or a cousin had to watch over their children. And when I needed more workers, the women brought in their family members to help out.

We *all* had to rely on our families in some way.

Yes, mixing business and family *can* get messy. Feelings get hurt, messages misinterpreted, grievances triggered. Look at what happened with Rudy and me. But all of that is okay. If we're working with family members we shouldn't put pressure on ourselves to make everything function perfectly, because it probably won't.

We need to embrace the messiness and accept it for what it is—the beautiful language of sharing our lives, love, and goals with the most important people we have.

I know one thing for sure—I wouldn't be a success today if I hadn't been able to lean on my family when I really needed them.

The same week that the last truck pulled out of the auto body shop with the Miracle Mops, Ronni and I drove the three hours to West Chester so I could go on the air at QVC.

I was exhausted. I was also really nervous. I had no idea if the interest in the mops would be great enough to satisfy Dan's order. What if they just didn't sell this time? What if we just sold a few thousand?

At the studio, I climbed up on the rotating stage, stared down the lights and the cameras, and I did what I had to do—I talked about the Miracle Mop from my heart.

In eight hours, we sold all 60,000 mops.

That very day, Dan placed an order for 60,000 more.

# 34

The Miracle Mop was a phenomenon. In business talk, it had wings. It was just one of those products that found its customers, and it kept finding them over and over again. Considering that so many people told me no one would ever buy a $20 mop, seeing it end up in hundreds of thousands of homes was more satisfying than I can even explain.

People saw what I saw—how the Miracle Mop was a unique product that could improve their lives. Maybe not in a huge way, but in a way that was meaningful, and in a way that really mattered.

I didn't decide that the Miracle Mop was a success, and neither did anyone at QVC.

The customers decided it. The customers always do.

And now, Dan had even bigger plans for the mop. He wanted me to keep manufacturing them for sale on QVC, but he also wanted to sell them through a direct response infomercial—one of those "1-800-Call Now!" ads on TV.

Infomercials traced back all the way to the start of TV itself, when shows were sponsored by a single company or product. In 1982, a company selling hair growth treatment coined the phrase "infomercial," and since then direct response infomercials have been used to sell everything from rotisseries to gym equipment to acne treatments. I loved the idea of reaching more people with the Miracle Mop, and I told Dan I'd do whatever he needed me to do.

I soon learned he didn't want me to do much.

I had a meeting with several QVC executives, including Dan and the young head of marketing at QVC, Mark Bozek. They explained the infomercial would be two minutes long and consist entirely of a model demonstrating the mop and a voice-over recorded by a man—the norm for every infomercial back then (you know, "It slices! It dices!" stuff like that). I said I didn't think that was the right way to sell the mop, but they were the experts.

"Women don't listen to women," they said.

That was a strange thing to say to the woman who'd just sold 60,000 Miracle Mops in a day.

Still, I wasn't in a position to dictate the terms of the infomercial. But I kept pushing for an ad that featured me talking about the Miracle Mop. I didn't give up until the producers agreed to shoot two versions of the commercial—one the way they wanted to do it, and one with me in it. They would air both of them over the same time period and compare results.

That sounded fair, until I realized they were basically humoring me. Almost all of the money in the production budget went to making their version. I would do mine on the rotating stage at QVC, on a backstage set while the front set was being used for a live segment.

The day of the shoot at QVC, I was more nervous than ever. It felt like I had to prove myself all over again, which was true. I'd picked one of the best QVC hosts, Jane Rudolph Treacy, to film the infomercial with me, and she helped me relax and feel more confident. When it was time to shoot, we climbed onto the kitchen set, each of us holding a Miracle Mop. The lights and cameras were all set up, and we were ready to go.

Suddenly, we heard, "Rotate!"

That wasn't supposed to happen.

Our set was supposed to stay in place long enough for us to shoot the infomercial. But suddenly we were on the move. I could see the camera wires being stretched tight while the overhead lights were getting yanked off the ceiling. Technicians were scrambling to take them down before they crashed to the ground. We were seconds away from a full-blown disaster when someone stopped the stage.

Okay, we were off to a great start.

We survived the shoot, and a few days later I sat down at QVC and watched the finished infomercial.

"Hi, I'm Joy, and I invented the Miracle Mop," I announced, kicking off a quick demonstration of the mop's many features. "You can use it in the bathroom, up the shower stall, behind the commode. This is literally the last mop you'll ever have to buy."

Then Jane wrapped it up by saying, "Why don't you give us a call. Our operators are standing by."

A few weeks later, I got a call from Dan Hardy.

"Okay, so we did the test of the two infomercials," he said.

There was a pause on the line. Inside, I was dying. All I could think was, *Okay, I guess we bombed.*

Always listen to the experts. The experts know what they're doing. Just listen and learn, and you'll be fine.

Why? Because people who've been doing something for a long time, and have been successful at it, know exactly what can and can't be done in that field.

Well, no. That's simply not true.

It's not true because *there are no experts*.

Even so-called "experts" can be wrong, and they often are. You will meet people who know more about a particular field than you—maybe even a lot more. Listen to them. Learn from them. But don't let them stop you from having your own opinion, and standing up for it.

Don't believe they know *everything* there is to know, because they don't. And guess what? You might even end up teaching the experts a thing or two.

Because in the end, an expert is only an expert until a better idea comes along, and that idea can come from anyone. Including you.

"Okay, Joy," Dan said on the phone, "we got the results back."

"Okay," I said, holding my breath.

"You were right. Your infomercial did better."

"Really?" I said.

"Yeah, uh, actually, it did ten times better."

The Miracle Mop infomercial broke ground in the field of direct response marketing. We proved you didn't need a traditional male voice-over to sell a good product. Before Jane and me, there hadn't been any

165

successful infomercials headlined by women. We showed there was a different way to do them—be real, be honest, talk directly to the customer. Our infomercial aired all across the country, and internationally, too. It aired at all hours, day after day after day, for years. It aired so often, people eventually got sick of seeing me on their TVs.

"Joy, if I hear your voice one more time," someone once came up to me and said, "I'm going to wring your hair instead of your mop."

In the world of retail, that means you're doing something right.

# 35

Let me tell you about the time I accidentally dropped a ten-ton boulder on a busy street in Long Island.

At Rudy's auto body shop, we kept cranking out Miracle Mops as fast as we could, and we even took over the shop's front offices. But as we got larger and larger orders for mops, one thing was clear—it was time to find a new place to make them.

It was time to find a real home for my company.

So I started looking for an office that wasn't directly adjacent to an active shooting range.

There was a new industrial complex in the nearby town of Edgewood, just five minutes from Rudy's shop, and I drove there to take a look. The first thing I noticed was that it was across the street from a miniature golf course.

That's when I knew I'd found the right place.

A few days later, I told the children we were all going to take a drive to look at my new office, which didn't exactly sound like an offer to go to Disneyland.

"Aw, Mom, do we have to?" one of them said.

"Yes, you do," I said, "because right afterward, we're all going to play miniature golf!"

That did the trick. And after that, the children always loved coming to see me at work so the four of us could sneak out and play miniature golf.

The office was four times the size of Rudy's auto body shop. By then, we had about forty looms that we used for the mop heads, and they were scattered all over Rudy's shop, tucked away in corners and hallways and wherever. But in my new headquarters, I had a big room where I could fit all forty looms with plenty of space to spare.

I had my own Loom Room!

There was one last thing I needed to make my new headquarters perfect. I needed a big rock.

I'd seen pictures of another office complex that had a massive boulder placed outside the front entrance, as a decorative touch. And I *loved* that. To me, a boulder would be a symbol of strength and permanence. So I went to a quarry on Long Island, and I picked out a beautiful slab of rock that glistened in the sun. It literally weighed ten tons. We arranged for a big crane to transport the stone to my office in Edgewood.

But on the way there, the crane driver went over some train tracks, which jostled the chains holding the stone in place, and all of a sudden the chains broke and the giant boulder fell off the crane and crashed down on the street.

No one was hurt, but traffic was seriously backed up for the next few hours. I'd like to apologize to every driver who got stuck behind my giant boulder that day.

In the end, my rock made it to Edgewood, where we perched it outside the front entrance. Over the years I've moved a few more times, and the rock comes with me everywhere I go.

Now I needed some new employees for my new company, which I called Ingenious Designs.

Two of my first official employees were my friend Ronni, and Richie from the shop. They'd been with me from the very beginning, and they had seen it all. Now they were moving with me to the new headquarters, where they would each have their own nice office. It felt like we were all graduating from college and heading into the real world together.

Early on, my mother Toots joined me at my new offices, too.

Toots had worked in several different offices, so she had plenty of experience in the business world. I asked her if she would come work with me, and she said yes. At the office, she sat in front and handled visitors and calls. I really enjoyed having her around, but there was one problem.

His name was Rudy.

By then I had paid back Rudy and Thelma every dollar I owed them, just as I'd promised. It took a long time, but I did it, and now my father was no longer involved in any big decisions. But he was still part of our daily goings-on. After all, we *had* been using his auto body shop. And sometimes he would help back up a delivery truck or something like that. If I got stuck, Rudy would even step in and babysit the children. I mean, he was my father, and no matter what he was a part of my life.

So when we moved out of the auto body shop and into my new offices, my father came along, too.

Having both Toots and Rudy in the office wasn't easy, and I knew it wouldn't be. I gave them offices as far away from each other as possible, which helped. Most of the time, Rudy ducked out the back door, avoiding Toots altogether. But sometimes he had to walk past her, and he'd jingle change in his pocket the way he always did, and Toots would roll her eyes as he walked by.

Sometimes it felt *exactly* the way it felt when Rudy showed up at our front door in East Meadow with suitcase in hand and moved into the basement, and I had to hide him down there every time Toots came to visit. It was like nothing had changed.

And you know what? I kind of liked it.

One morning, I took Bobby to one of his hockey games at a local rink in Long Island. Actually, it was more like the middle of the night. Kids play hockey early in the suburbs; Bobby's game was at 5:00 a.m. That meant I had to get up at 3:00 a.m., make breakfast for Bobby, dress him up in his bulky hockey uniform, pack him into the car like a giant hockey marshmallow, and get him to the rink on time, all while trying not to fall asleep.

We made it on time, and the first mother I bumped into at the rink was Jan—my old friend and co-worker from Eastern Air Lines! The one who had an even worse old car than me!

Jan was there with her son Chris. We hadn't seen each other in years, and we sat down and talked and caught up, and I told her all about the Miracle Mop. Jan was talented in a lot of ways, and at the time she was working as a graphic artist.

"Boy, if I only had you to help me with designing the packaging," I said.

Not much later, Jan started working at my company, too. She wound up handling everything—marketing, packaging, graphic design, you name it. She was also in charge of preparing all the sets I used at QVC. Jan was indispensable. I guess we'd both come a long way since we'd had to warm our freezing fingers in an airport bathroom.

The next person I hired might surprise you.

After Tony and I got divorced, he got remarried a few years later. But Tony was still a presence in my life, and we got along fine. He'd pick up the children one day on most weekends and take them out to have fun. Sometimes he'd be late, and the children would sit on the front step for hours, playing the "guess-which-color-the-next-car-will-be" game.

But when Tony did show up, it was like the circus was in town. He'd sweep up the kids and take them to a Mets game or ice skating or Adventureland or Chuck E. Cheese or the movies, and no matter where they went they always had the most fun time with him.

Once in a while, when Tony brought the children back home, he'd pop inside to say hello, and we'd chat for a bit. Other times he'd write out a child support check on the hood of the car and have Bobby bring it to me. We were never mean to each other, but I guess we weren't overly friendly, either.

Tony was still working for Wise. He'd been there for fifteen years and he was one of their most senior salesmen. He was still taking clients to baseball games and on fishing trips, and he was still known as the King of Entertainment. Tony liked the job and he was really good at it. One thing Tony could do was sell. He could sell you anything.

Well, it just so happened that I needed a salesman.

As my business grew, I needed someone who could help get our products into stores. Having QVC was great, but there were so many more people I wanted to reach. I needed someone I knew and trusted, someone I could lean on, to help me expand that reach.

Who better, I thought, than Tony?

One day when Tony brought the children back, I pulled him aside.

"Tony, I want you to come work for me," I said.

"Huh?" he said. "You want me to what?"

"I want you to come work for my company."

"Why would I ever do that?"

We sat down and I explained my thinking.

"If you come here, and we find a way to make it work, it will benefit all of us," I said. "You, me, and the kids. You'll see them more and they'll love having you around. And I need a great salesman, which you are."

The end of our marriage had been tough, but we both understood why it happened. Tony came to the same realization I did—that we were two very different people who weren't going to be happy married. I was a stay-at-home person. I liked reading books and decorating the house and waking up early. Tony was a night owl. He craved excitement and activity. We broke apart because we weren't meant to be together.

But just because we weren't meant to be together as husband and wife didn't mean we couldn't still be part of each other's lives. No matter what, we always would be *major* parts of each other's lives, because of the children. Couldn't our relationship evolve into something different? Tony wasn't a great husband for me, but did that mean he couldn't be important to me in other ways? And vice versa?

I always believed there was something very special about Tony, and that didn't change after we got divorced. I felt like I knew the very best (and the very worst) parts of him, and I always felt like he was *supposed* to be in my life. Our connection was based on something that was very resilient and enduring. When we met he wasn't ready to be a great husband or father.

But I believed he was ready now to be a good friend and confidant.

I respected what Tony did. He was a very good salesman. But I was a pretty good salesperson, too, and Tony knew that, and he respected that, too. There was nothing charitable about what either of us would be doing. It would just be a new relationship that I believed could work.

Tony thought about everything I said.

And he said yes.

Tony's first few months at Ingenious Designs were difficult, because he still didn't get along with Rudy. The sound of Rudy jingling change still drove him crazy. I gave them offices in opposite corners, too (and yes, I was running out of corners).

Now it really did feel like the old days.

One day, Rudy showed up at the office with a motorized scooter, and he gave the children rides up and down the hallways. A few days later, I caught him throwing something at a vendor in anger. Then Tony would get mad at Rudy, or Rudy would get mad at Toots, or Toots would shout at me down the hallway instead of using the intercom, or all of them would be arguing about something, and pretty much every day there was some family squabble or skirmish that just made me laugh.

I mean, how could I not laugh? I'd brought everyone together again, so I had no one to blame but myself.

Luckily, things between Rudy and Tony settled down a little bit. And I was right—the children *loved* having Tony there, and having him in their lives a little more.

Since coming on board, Tony has been part of all the successes and setbacks and special moments connected to the business. He helped us line up new clients and vendors and expand the business into retail. He was always able to finesse a tricky business situation so that everyone walked away from it feeling like a million bucks. And he was a really good sounding board for me—someone I could bounce things off and get an honest opinion in return. Having Tony there increased my comfort level by a lot.

And despite all the warnings I got about hiring my ex-husband, it all worked out just fine. Recently, Tony passed the twentieth anniversary of coming to work with me.

That's ten years longer than we stayed married!

And all because I circled back and took another look.

I know that bringing Tony back was not a conventional thing to do. But for me, it was the right thing to do.

Tony was a hero to me—he changed my life for the better, and forever. He gave me three amazing children, the loves of my life. He brought an excitement and vibrancy to my world that I hadn't even known I'd been missing. Even after our divorce, we had a level of love and trust for each other that was special and unique.

All I had to do was circle back to Tony and look at our relationship in a different way. And I had to be open to our relationship taking on a new and different form. And I was. I embraced both the good and bad things about Tony, because what was good about him was meaningful to me. He was a good father, and our children loved him dearly, and they wanted to be with him as much as they could. There was a special value for me in having Tony in our life, and so I found a way to make it possible.

I circled back with Tony, and I'm very glad that I did.

In business and in life, I believe it's important for us to keep circling back to people, rather than cutting them out of our lives.

Keeping my dreams and goals intertwined with the dreams and goals of my family and friends—and always looking for the best in them instead of the worst—has allowed me to keep my little gang together for a long, long time.

Has it been messy at times? Yes.

But it's also been really, really beautiful.

# 36

The success of the Miracle Mop changed my life. It was the beginning of my rebirth into a more confident, creative person. It allowed me to trust my instincts even more. For a long time, I couldn't even bring myself to tell people that I was an inventor. If they asked me what I did, I'd always answer, "I'm the mother of three children." Which was true, because that will always be my most important job.

But I just didn't feel comfortable saying I was an inventor.

Over time, that began to change. My confidence in my ideas and my vision grew and grew. You know how, if you saw a friend walking with bare feet over sharp little rocks, you'd feel very confident in concluding that they needed to put on shoes? Well, *that's* how confident I was becoming about my ideas for new products and new creations—as if it was obvious that they needed to exist.

Which, to me, it was.

For the first time in a long time, I felt free to think about new products and new ways to make a difference in people's lives. So I went to all kinds of stores, attended trade shows, and just really tried to keep my eyes open for any new idea or new inspiration. At one trade show, I noticed an item by a company from Holland. It was a little roll-up storage kit you could use for organizing knickknacks and things like that. You rolled it out to see everything in its compartment, and you rolled it back up to store it away.

And then, in an instant, it hit me. Two simple words.

Junk drawer.

Everyone has a junk drawer. You know, the drawer you throw everything into that has nowhere else to go. Pens, pencils, batteries, beads, ribbons, spools of thread, Band-Aids, Matchbox cars, anything. And when you open it up, everything jangles and clangs around and you can't find the one thing you absolutely must find at that very moment in order to keep your family from running off the rails.

The junk drawer.

But what if everything we keep in our junk drawers could be rolled up and tucked neatly away in one place? Not in a bag that can topple and spill over, or a drawer that can be pulled out too far and scatter a million tiny items under the sofa. No—a sturdy rolling kit that can be put away safely, snug and secure.

What if I could get rid of the junk drawer?

I took the idea to QVC, and they gave me the go-ahead. I contacted the patent holders in Holland, and we signed a deal to remake the kits based on my improvements to their design, using the same plastic we used for the Miracle Mop. They sent us their molds, and at my new warehouse we set up more assembly tables right next to the ones we used to make the mops.

Then we got to work, and the Rolykit was born.

Right away, people got it. They understood it. They saw the same thing I did in my mind. I guess I wasn't the only one with a junk drawer problem. The Rolykit became one of QVC's best-selling products. It sold out pretty much every time I went on the air with it. I made a second Rolykit designed for children in bright colors, and called it the RolyPoly Kit, because that's what my children called it.

As the months and years passed, the Rolykit just kept going. The orders got bigger and bigger, and Mark Bozek filmed another infomercial with me. This time, we did all the credit card processing and shipping right out of my new office. Ronni ran that operation, along with our newest helper—my son Bobby.

One time, QVC put in a really big order for more Rolykits—so big that it kind of took me by surprise. I had more workers than ever before, but we were still understaffed, particularly for huge orders that had to be filled quickly. Before I knew it my Rolykit deadline arrived, and I had to assemble thousands of kits in a single night.

So I did what I'd always done before—I leaned on my family.

I asked Christie to bring all the girls from her high school cheerleading squad and all the boys from the baseball team to the warehouse to help us out. I asked Bobby to bring his friends from his softball team, too. Even Jackie brought her friends along. We all met at the warehouse on a Friday after school, and we formed a big assembly line, and for the next several hours we put thousands of molded parts together on a conveyer belt, so they could be connected into Rolykits.

It was an amazing night. The kids played loud music, and everyone was laughing, and Bobby took breaks to toss a baseball around the warehouse with Christie's friends. Everyone got paid and we ordered pizzas— more pizzas than I'd ever ordered at one time.

I probably would have saved money by hiring regular workers, with how much pizza these guys ate.

But it was worth it. You know how I feel about having my family around. We all worked through the night, and by early the next morning, all of the Rolykits were done.

The Rolykits were so successful, I decided to create a brand-new product using the same roll-up design—a beautiful, luxurious, multi-compartment jewelry box.

Jewelry clutter was another problem I knew too well. Keeping rings and chains and bracelets separate and organized was almost impossible. How many times did I have to untangle two necklaces that didn't want to come apart?

But what if I could design a small box that featured elegant, velvety trays, like the ones they have in fancy department stores, but that also rolled up and allowed you to keep your necklaces away from each other and your rings and bracelets from getting all jumbled up? What if all your jewelry stayed put because of the way the velvet trays rolled up?

The prototype we created was stunning. The smooth exterior was a shiny black, and when you opened the top you saw a deep compartment covered with a rich, dark velvety fabric, and a mirror that flipped to just the right angle. There were little slots on one side of it where you could arrange your rings and keep them separate. When you unrolled each side, there were more deep, velvety trays. Every piece of jewelry you stored in this box would fit snugly into its own space and be rolled up and perfectly protected.

All of your most valued possessions, safe, sound, and organized.

I took the prototype to QVC, and they loved it. Especially Jeff Tara-schi, who at the time was running QVC's booming jewelry division. Jeff was brilliant and energetic and contagiously positive, as well as aggressive and confident in his instincts.

Jeff put in an order for 50,000 Jewel Kits. *50,000!*

That left me with around six months to create, box, and ship 50,000 units. That was a pretty tight schedule, but not impossible. That is, as long as everything went smoothly.

Everything did not go smoothly.

The biggest challenge was the velvety trays. They had to be created through a process called flocking. Flocking a flat surface was easy, but our trays weren't flat, they were sunken and rounded. Nothing we tried worked right.

Several times Jan and I had to fly to Wisconsin, where the trays were being made, to inspect the molds and trays. Each time we'd meet the engineers at the airport, look at the trays, point out all the problems, then get right back on a plane to New York. Two months passed—a third of the way through our production schedule—and we still hadn't manufactured a single tray. We didn't even know *how* to make them yet.

Around then, I got a call from Jeff Taraschi.

"Joy!" he said. "How's it going?"

"Great!" I answered. "It's going great!"

"You'll make the deadline, right?"

"Of course we will!"

"Okay! Go get 'em!"

I flew to Wisconsin again, this time to visit the factory. There, I found two workers assembling ten trays. Ten trays! I had to deliver 50,000 Jewel Kits in three months! That night in my hotel room, Jeff called again.

"Joy!" he said. "How we doing with the kits?"

"Jeff, we're doing just great," I said.

"You know, you were supposed to be shipping your first wave of kits already. Is everything okay?"

"Everything's fine! Everything's great. We're right where we need to be."

"Okay! Keep me posted!"

I finally had to switch to a new facility. I flew to the new plant in Wisconsin and I laid down the law.

"Guys, we *have* to start manufacturing these kits right now," I told the workers there. "Let's roll up our sleeves and work out a schedule and stick to it."

Right away, one of the workers told me the plant would be closed the following week. Not for a day or two—the whole week. I didn't understand what he meant.

"Why would the plant be shut for a whole week?" I asked.

"Hunting season," he replied.

I thought he might be joking. He wasn't.

"We really need to keep the plant open," I said, half pleading, half insisting.

"Sorry," the worker said. "It's hunting season."

Sure enough, the plant stayed closed that week. Because it was hunting season.

In the end, we were only able to ship 25,000 Jewel Kits to QVC in time for the first show. Only half the order. That wasn't a minor inconvenience, it was a major problem. In the product business, you simply have to have enough product to sell, and half orders just don't cut it. Inventory is fuel. Without it, you just can't fly.

Thankfully, when I finally went on the air to talk about the Jewel Kit, our customers loved them. We sold all 25,000 kits the very first morning. Jeff was right—we could have easily sold the full 50,000 order, and then some.

After the Jewel Kit, I just kept going. I created a bucket for the Miracle Mop that held it upright with its handle, so the mop wouldn't scrape your wall when you dropped it to answer the phone (that was the Tuck-it Bucket). I made a travel mirror with a built-in, flexible arm, so you could unwind it anywhere (the Handy Hook Mirror). And I came up with the Piatto Bakery Box while having ice cream with my children.

And yet, the success of my products did not change the basic reality of my life—that every new product I created had to be successful, or else I'd be out of business.

The nature of what I was doing required me to put so much money into creating the products, and if any of them didn't sell well, I'd be in deep financial trouble. I had no margin for error.

Every decision I made was make-or-break.

Including my next decision, which was to make a product most people told me had absolutely no chance of success.

# 37

I was in Paris, filming shows there for QVC, when on a break I wandered into a very chic, very high-end clothing store. I was just browsing, because there was no way I could afford a single thing in the store. The gown that really caught my eye, for instance, cost around $10,000. It was draped on a special hanger that was extra thick and had a bit of velvet fabric wrapped around it on the ends, which kept the pricey gown from slipping off.

And then—BOOM.

It hit me.

*Why don't we have hangers like this in our closets?*

The beautiful, thick, velvety hanger in the Paris store cost $100. Imagine that—a $100 hanger. But the velvety fabric really did keep the expensive gown from slipping off.

What if I could find a way to make a nonslip hanger that everyone could afford, and that could be helpful to all of us, not just high-end couturiers in Paris?

I sat down and started thinking about hangers and closets. Okay, so what was wrong with our closets? Well, our hangers, for a start. They were usually made of wood or wire or plastic, and all of those surfaces could be slippery. Clothes fall off hangers all the time, especially when we jostle them around in an overstuffed closet.

And hangers were always mismatched, with clunky, thick wood ones next to cheap wire ones next to fragile plastic ones, all of it adding up to some stressful mornings.

But what if I put something on the hanger to hold the clothing in place? Not velvet, which would be too expensive, but something like the velvety flocking we used for the Jewel Kits?

And what if I made the hanger much thinner than the thick hanger in the Paris store? Thinner than those thick wooden hangers that eat up so much space in our closets?

And what if I made the ends gently curved, so there would be no ugly shoulder bumps on our sweaters?

And what if I made the hangers affordable enough so that everyone could get them, and we'd never want to use those awful dry-cleaning wire hangers ever again?

That's what was going on in my brain in that store as I stood and stared at a hanger. Not the dress—the hanger.

As soon as I got back to Long Island, I went to work on a curved, ultrathin, ultra durable, velvety flocked hanger. I found the idea so incredibly exciting. It would help people like me unclutter our closets and take more control over our lives. But as soon as I began describing it to people, I got a lot of blank looks. Most people were baffled by why I'd want to spend so much time worrying about a hanger.

"Joy, no one is interested in hangers," they'd say.

Even Bobby said, "Mom, hangers are free. Why would anybody buy a hanger?"

Apparently, in the hierarchy of boring household items, hangers were even lower than mops. The way people reacted, it seemed like I couldn't have picked a less exciting, less important product to work on. People simply didn't see the point.

But I did. I saw it clearly. I believed I was onto something that could improve people's lives in a very real way. A new and better hanger.

I called them the Huggable Hangers.

Creating the hangers, not surprisingly, was a long and complicated process. Flocking was a major challenge again. But we got them made, and I brought them to the executives at QVC.

"Joy, these are just hangers," one executive told me. "We don't sell hangers here."

"No, no, no, people will love them," I kept having to say. "You'll see. This is going to be incredible."

No matter how hard I tried, I couldn't convince anyone the hangers would be a hit. But I just kept assuring everyone that people would love the hangers. I knew in my heart that they would. QVC put in a very small order and they let me go on the air with them late at night. As a courtesy.

And then . . .

. . . we fizzled. We sold some Huggable Hangers, but not nearly enough.

It was my first disappointing performance at QVC. The truth was, we weren't quite ready. We didn't even have a makeshift closet on the set; instead, we'd borrowed one of those bellman's carts from a hotel nearby, and we hung all the hangers on the cart. I talked about all the benefits of the hanger: its size, its sturdiness, the velvety finish, the extra room we'd have in our closets—everything that made it a great hanger.

But we just never really connected with consumers.

Personally, I took it hard. I was used to creating phenomenally successful products, and this time I had failed to do that. And failure is tough. Failure is heartbreaking. Failure can make us want to give up.

But failure, if you think about it, is just another experience in our lives.

And in life, every single experience we have—every single moment—is something we can learn from, and use to push us forward.

I look at failure as the chance to fill up my basket with resources. All the hard lessons I learn by failing make me stronger and leave me better prepared to handle the next challenge.

Some people are so afraid of failing, they will avoid all challenges and risks and confrontations. They think about the downside of what could happen, and that's enough to scare them away from even trying.

But that's something else I've learned—the downside isn't always a downside. For instance, if the only downside is that we'll feel embarrassed and ridiculed if we fail in our endeavor, I don't believe that's enough of a downside to get in the way of us trying.

In fact, the downside can actually be an upside! The most successful people in business, and in life, learn from everything that happens to them, even the really bad, painful things. They don't shy away from confrontation and interaction, they *crave* it. They know the experience, positive or negative, will be transformative. And so they keep their eyes open for every new experience, and they don't let the possible downside stop them.

Because a lot of the time, the worst thing that can happen if we fail is that we get to fill up our baskets with resources, and we become stronger and more resilient, and that makes us even more powerful heading into whatever incredible challenge comes next.

So let's take a deeper look at the downside. Because the downside isn't always a downside.

# 38

Not long after I launched the Huggable Hangers, I got a call from Mark Bozek, the young marketing executive I worked with at QVC. Mark had since moved on to become the President of HSN, the rival home shopping network to QVC.

"Joy, come into the office to see us," Mark said. "Talk to Barry. He wants you to come to HSN."

Barry, I knew, was Barry Diller, the CEO of HSN, and one of the most powerful media moguls in the country. Apparently, Barry wanted me to come to HSN.

HSN? The competitor?

I waffled a little with Mark on the phone. But he was persuasive and I finally agreed to a meeting.

By then, Barry Diller was already a legend in the business. He had dropped out of UCLA after one semester, went to work in the William

Morris mailroom, and climbed his way up from there. He ran Paramount Pictures for ten years, and 20th Century Fox for several more. He also became CEO of QVC, though we never had the chance to meet when he was there.

Barry left QVC and in 1997 bought HSN. He had an incredible amount of money and financial backing, and his goal was to build the company of the future—a conglomerate of exciting new ventures like Expedia and Ticketmaster and Lending Tree. The crown jewel of his mega-company would be HSN.

And he wanted me to be part of it.

I went by myself to meet Barry and Mark in Barry's office. He may have been one of the most powerful men in the world of media, but in his office that day Barry came across as a friendly guy you knew from around the neighborhood. The meeting was low-key and amiable. Barry asked me about my business, my products, my vision for the future.

"So where are you going now?" he asked. "Where do you *want* to go?"

I said I wanted to keep inventing great products that help people.

Then Barry got serious.

"Joy, we are going to build HSN into the biggest TV retail experience in the world. And we want you to be a part of it. We don't want to just sell your products. We want you. We want you to be a partner with HSN, and to be an executive of the company, so you can have a say in how things go. We can fund your business and support your marketing and sales appearances, and you can focus on doing what you love most. Making amazing products."

I smiled. Barry was exactly right. That *was* what I loved doing most.

But was HSN the best place for me to keep doing it?

I went home and thought a lot about my situation. The harsh reality was that every new invention I came up with required an enormous expenditure of time and energy and money just to get to the point where I could have it ready to sell.

And if it didn't do well, it could be the end of the road for me as an inventor.

Every new product I created was a huge risk. Every one. The Miracle Mop. The Rolykits. The Jewel Kit. The Piatto Bakery Box. Each one of them represented a make-or-break moment for me. And it wasn't just me assuming that risk. It was my children, too.

My future, and the future of my family, was always on the line.

So what I needed most of all was a place where I could continue to create great products for consumers, but also take away a little bit of the risk.

As an executive at HSN, I would be part of a team. I'd have access to HSN's marketing people, their graphic designers, their researchers—lots of different people who could help take some of the burden off me. Moving to HSN could give me more freedom, and more power, to do what I really loved—make new things.

Moving to HSN made sense. It made a lot of sense.

But before I made a decision, there was someone I had to talk to.

I wrote a long letter to Dan Hardy at QVC, telling him about Barry's offer. I felt a sense of loyalty to Dan. He believed in me and he took a big chance by putting me on the air. Dan was brilliant at what he did and I learned a lot from him. When it came to products, he knew instantly what would work and what wouldn't. He wasn't flashy or loud, but you could tell he was always in control. I respected him, and I was thankful to him. He played a really big part in my life.

Now, I wanted to see if Dan would consider a situation like the deal Barry proposed.

Dan's answer was no. He said he didn't want me to leave QVC, but he wanted to keep things the way they were.

I understood that. But for me, the chance to take a creative step forward—to reinvent my life, in a way—was simply too good to pass up.

The next person I talked to was Tony. Not my ex-husband, Tony, but a different Tony—my personal lawyer and dearest friend, Tony Curto.

Tony Curto was an incredible man. He grew up in Brooklyn, around the corner from Barbra Streisand. His parents came over from Italy, and he was the first person in his family to go to college. He got through law school in two years and became a top business attorney, working for Coca-Cola and other huge companies. He was the person I always turned to when I needed help making a plan to get something done.

Tony was my Answer Man.

When I told him about the HSN offer, he asked me how much I thought my company was worth.

I told him the dollar figure I had in mind.

Tony got quiet. Clearly, he thought my number was too high. *Way* too high. Tony was experienced with price/earnings ratios and balance sheets, and he told me the number I gave him wasn't realistic.

But I didn't want to change it. To me, it was a fair number. I knew what it was worth. I trusted my gut instinct. Tony finally came around, but he had one more bit of advice. He told me I should ask for even more.

"That gives you a fallback position," he said. "Bargaining is about movement and accommodation."

I thought about that for a minute.

"No, just ask for my number," I finally said. "That's what I want."

"Okay, how about we ask for just a little bit more?"

"No, just my number. Tell them they can take it or leave it."

"Joy, you have to give them room to negotiate. That's the normal course of any business deal."

I was so sure of what I wanted to do, I made a bet with Tony. I said, "I will bet you a dime that if they're going to partner with me, they're going to do it for the price I walk in and ask for."

I didn't want to play games. I wanted to be as straightforward as I could be. I always spoke straight from my heart, whether I was on the air or in a boardroom or at the supermarket. This might not have been a good negotiating tactic with HSN, but that's just who I was. Tony understood that, and when he went to see HSN's lawyers, he asked for exactly the amount I wanted.

The reaction from the lawyers was—nothing.

No reaction. Zero.

"That was even worse than astonishment or a flat no," Tony would later say. "It meant they considered it a nonsense number."

In his second meeting with HSN, after he and the lawyers had gone over a number of other issues, one of them turned to Tony and said, "Okay, so what is the number that Joy wants?"

Tony repeated my asking price.

This time, he got a reaction. Eyebrows were raised. People shifted uncomfortably in their seats. There were frowns.

Then came the third meeting. The negotiations were intense now. Patents, protections, inventory, sales numbers—the nitty-gritty of the deal. The head HSN lawyer looked Tony in the eye and said, "Okay, now we're serious. What is the real number Joy wants?"

Once again, Tony repeated my asking price.

In the end, Tony closed the deal for exactly what I wanted.

And he kicked in the dime he owed me, too.

Ten years after the launch of the Miracle Mop, I moved to HSN.

Late one night, after I'd put in an extremely long day, Bobby woke up and got out of bed and found me sitting at the kitchen table, totally exhausted. He looked at me earnestly with his big brown eyes and made a declaration.

"Mom, I think you're working too hard," Bobby said. "I'm worried that you're killing yourself."

I hugged him close and assured him I was fine. And I wasn't lying. I *was* fine. I was exhausted, but I was okay. Actually, I was much more than okay. I was great! Really, really great! And all because of one simple, undeniable fact.

I loved what I was doing.

I mean, I loved it. I really and truly loved it. And I still do. Maybe not every second of it, or even every day of it, but just about.

Many years later, when Bobby was all grown up, he told me, "Joy, I never realized how much you love your work. How much you love the *nuts and bolts* of it."

Bobby's right—I do love the nuts and bolts of it. I love every part of the creative process, even the parts that are really hard—maybe *especially* those parts. Sometimes I say that I can't wait to go to sleep, because I can't wait to get up in the morning. And believe me, I know how lucky that makes me.

What I've learned is that life is not a lottery. Success isn't an end point—it's just a new beginning.

Moving to HSN only meant I'd have to keep doing what I was doing, and do even *more* of it. Success will put you on a track to keep doing whatever it is that made you successful.

So you better decide to do something you truly love doing.

I often hear people say, "Oh, this is just my job, but what I'm really passionate about is this other thing." But what if the thing that excited us most was also the thing that made us successful? What if our definition of success was not how much money we made, but how much we loved doing the thing we did every day?

I'm not saying it's an easy thing to pull off. But I sincerely believe it's a goal worth chasing. It's out there, and it's real. That's why I made the move to HSN—because it gave me the chance to do even more of what I love doing. Of what truly *ignites* me as a human being.

To me, that is the definition of success—finding our passion, and making it the driving force of our lives.

One of the first things I did when I made the move to HSN was put the Huggable Hangers back on air.

This time, the hotel bellman's cart was gone. Instead, I had closets built on the set. People could see how the hanger created more space—three times more space—and how a messy, overstuffed closet turned into a tidy, half-filled oasis just by switching to Huggable Hangers.

This time, I did it right.

And guess what? People got it. They saw what I saw. They got on their phones and called in. And they bought Huggable Hangers. A lot of people bought a lot of hangers. After one day of selling them, Barry sent me a note saying I'd shattered the previous record for single-day sales at HSN, by a lot.

I always believed the Huggable Hanger was a product that would make our lives better.

And the customers proved it.

Today, we're coming up on one billion hangers sold.

One. Billion. Hangers.

The Huggable Hangers weren't just a hit.

They were a *phenomenon*.

# PART
# THREE

*"I SEE OBJECTS THAT AREN'T THERE.*

*I SOLVE PROBLEMS NO ONE ASKS ME TO SOLVE.*

*I'M AN INVENTOR, AND I MAKE THINGS."*

JOY MANGANO

# 39

In most Hollywood movies, this is the part where the hero rides off into the sunset and the credits roll. But if you know anything about me by now, you know that's not really my style.

It's true that the deal with HSN changed my life in many magical ways. After so many years of scrimping and scraping and putting just about every dollar back into my business, I was secure, financially, for the first time in my life, and that was an incredible feeling.

I was, for example, finally able to trade up from my beat-up old white Lumina minivan to, eventually, a brand-new white Range Rover. It's certainly safer, and it's got a lot of great technology, but really, I just love driving it—especially to Vermont, where I still love to ski.

I also put away enough money to fund all my children's educations. And my grandchildren's educations. And my grandchildren's grandchildren's educations.

And I finally bought my dream house—a 40,000-square-foot fixer-upper that had been abandoned for years on the North Shore of Long Island. I've always dreamed of getting a big house that I could fix and decorate exactly how I wanted, and I did just that. There's enough room for all my children and all their families to stay over at the same time, which is part of what makes it my dream house. And yes, the floors are spotless and the closets are filled with Huggable Hangers.

But the truth is, I didn't see my move to HSN as a chance to slow down or bask in my glory. I saw it as a chance to reinvent myself again. I saw it as a chance to do what I love to do, but at a higher level, and with a greater impact.

I saw it this way because I believed that what I was doing truly mattered to people like me.

So instead of retiring or putting my life on cruise control, I doubled down. I started working even harder and stretching even further. I believed with all my heart that my ideas could help people across the country live a life that was just a little better, and just a little brighter.

And you know what? Two years after I joined HSN, my business doubled.

And then it doubled again.

And then again.

And again.

In the seventeen years since I moved to HSN, I grew my business not by a factor of two, or three, or even ten.

I grew it by a factor of twenty-five.

And boy, has my life changed!

I'm now appearing on HSN at least once a month, beamed into over 90 million homes, and I'm widely regarded as the most successful and respected inventor in my industry. My products are also carried in major nationwide retailers like Macy's, Meijer, Target, Lowe's, Bed Bath & Beyond, and The Container Store.

And the best part? I get to follow my ideas wherever they lead me, with no limits or boundaries or barriers.

How did I do it?

The answer is simple.

By trusting my instincts, relying on those closest to me, and never ever forgetting what got me here in the first place.

Dreams. Ideas. And family.

# 40

"Joy, I've got this great idea for a product, can I tell you about it?"

I hear this all the time. *All* the time. A makeup artist told me about a new kind of airbrush she'd invented while I was in her makeup chair. And a greeter at Home Depot ran up to me and said, "Joy! My wife has this really great idea, let me tell you all about it!"

That's what makes this world an amazing place—anyone can have an idea, and any one of those ideas can have a very real impact.

As my business grew, I wasn't just approached by makeup artists and guys at Home Depot. I started getting requests from celebrities and famous artists who wanted my help in figuring out a path to share their product ideas with the world.

But here's the thing—in my career I became famous for inventing products. I never invented products simply because I was famous (and you'd be surprised by how often that happens).

So before I partnered with any celebrity, I made one thing clear to myself, and to everyone who worked with me—the most important thing was not the fame of the celebrity, or the buzz surrounding the project, but rather the quality and uniqueness and usefulness of the product that we would create together.

One of the very first celebrities I met with was the supermodel Iman. When she scheduled a lunch with me, I didn't really know what to expect. I guess I didn't know how committed she would be to her ideas or products. As I said, I was very careful about working with celebrities.

But then I met Iman, and all that changed.

She was strikingly beautiful and incredibly strong-willed, but she was also clearly passionate and deeply knowledgeable about the products in her field. She came prepared with illustrated boards and business plans and fabric swatches and clothing samples. She put on a show right there in the restaurant, and it was dazzling.

Iman explained how she'd been on the covers of literally thousands of fashion magazines, and how she had learned the fashion business inside and out, starting from the bottom and working her way to the top. She had a clear vision for her future—she wanted to create a line of beautiful, quality handbags and clothing that would be accessible to everyone.

I was impressed. Her ideas made sense to me. And I saw how they could improve people's lives in meaningful ways. The passion was there. The commitment was there. And most importantly, the product was there. Iman struck me as a true artist. Not long after that lunch, we agreed to work together.

And Iman built one of the most successful fashion brands on all of HSN.

Not much later, I had the opportunity to create an infomercial for a beautiful new kitchen product. The infomercial would feature a very famous celebrity chef who had worked with us in the past. But then, at the very last minute, the chef dropped out.

I had a production crew in place, and a studio rented, and everything was ready to go, so I had to really scramble or else I'd lose it all (can't anything just run smoothly for once?).

Then—I had an idea.

A few months earlier, I'd met a chef named Ming Tsai at a Chicago trade show. He had his own PBS show, and he was creative and charismatic and exceptionally gifted. I remember thinking then that our paths would cross again.

So, the night before we were set to film, I pulled Chef Ming's number up on my cell phone and called him. Then I asked him if he would be interested in helping me launch a new carving knife called the Aero Knife.

"When do you need me?" he asked.

I took a deep breath.

"Tomorrow morning," I said.

There was a silence on the other end. A long silence.

"I'll do it," Chef Ming finally said, "but only if the product is really great."

That's when I knew I'd made the right call.

I drew up a quick two-page contract and faxed it to Chef Ming to sign. I got him on an early morning flight to Tampa, and we filmed the commercial right on schedule. Chef Ming had remarkable, world-class knife skills, and they were on full display. The Aero Knife went on to become a huge hit, and today his Simply Ming line of products is one of HSN's largest culinary brands.

It was a hot summer day in Nashville, and I was sitting next to Keith Urban. Yes, the world-famous singer and entertainment superstar. We enjoyed a nice lunch together. I had a sandwich and a few skipped heartbeats (Keith is also one of the most charming men around).

We were having a lunch meeting to discuss the possibility of working together. I asked Keith if he'd ever thought of creating his own line of guitars.

"Joy, that's my dream," Keith said. "But guitars are either too expensive or not great quality. And what I want to do is give *everyone* the chance to pick up a quality guitar and learn how to play."

"Keith, I can help you with that," I said. "That's what I do."

I worked with Keith to perfect a new kind of guitar. *His* kind of guitar. The guitar neck was thinner and easier to hold, while the strings were closer to the fret board and easier to push down. The strings were also comfort-coated, so they didn't hurt your fingertips. It was a beautiful guitar, it was affordable, and it was something we believed would bring the joy of playing music to a lot of people.

But that wasn't enough for Keith. He wanted to do more.

Keith wanted to create a series of lessons in which he personally taught people how to play the guitar. Keith didn't want to teach complex theory, he wanted to teach *songs*—which was exactly how he learned to play. And so he sat alone in front of the cameras and crew, guitar in hand, for hour after hour, day after day, talking thoughtfully and patiently about his approach to music. It was intimate and genius and a feat of pure love and devotion.

It took nearly two months, but Keith created thirty full-length lessons. The final package, the Player Guitar Series by Keith Urban, and his

30 Songs in 30 Days lessons series, went on to teach millions of lessons to aspiring guitarists all over the country. And it anchored the No. 1 infomercial program in our entire industry.

The theme of my career, and a guiding principle behind everything I do, is something that's so simple it's easy to forget.

Product is King.

It doesn't matter who you are or where you came from—if you make a truly great product, people will find it. If you make an amazing hot dog, people will flock to your hot dog stand. Trust me, I've seen it happen.

This is perhaps the one indisputable truth of my business—if your product is exceptional and innovative and meaningful to people's lives, they will line up for what you make.

On the flip side, if you've got a great reputation or you're wealthy or famous, but your product isn't all that great, people are not going to love it.

It won't matter how celebrated or adored you are, or how much glitter and gloss you wrap yourself up in—if you aren't giving people what they truly need and deserve in their lives, then you're just not going to succeed.

This isn't only true in business—it's just as true in life.

We all have unique skills and exceptional talents, and we all have something extraordinary to share with the world. We are all capable of adding great beauty to the lives of the people around us.

But in order for that to happen, what we offer to the world *has* to be authentic, and it *has* to be the very best that it can be. Whatever it is—our parenting, our friendship, our support, our laughter, or our love—we have to bring a fierce devotion to making our "product" great.

Not just okay, and not just good, and not just really good.

It has to be the very best product we can offer the world.

And if we do that, in business and in life, we will be successful.

When I was in Hawaii recently, a mother and father came up to me at a restaurant and asked me if their young daughter could share her idea with me. I said of course, and they ushered their daughter forward toward my table. She was so nervous she was trembling, but she took a deep breath and in a soft voice she told me her idea.

And you know what? It was a pretty good idea.

It didn't matter that she was so young. It didn't matter that she was nervous, or that we were in a restaurant in Hawaii. All that mattered was that her idea was a good idea. That's all that ever matters.

I gave the girl a hug and I told her what I tell everyone who comes up to me with an idea. I told her to remember three simple words.

Product is King.

# 41

You'll always hear me say, "I can't wait to go to bed at night, so I can wake up again in the morning."

I say that a lot because I get to live my dream life every day. And it's not about money or fame, though those are very nice things to have. It's about having the freedom to turn my ideas into reality, and then watch them impact the world. That is what makes me so excited to get up every morning.

*That's* what makes me feel successful.

So when I moved to HSN, and I gained even more freedom to explore new ideas and make great products, I felt an incredible surge of creative energy.

I couldn't *wait* to get started.

People often ask me, "Joy, how do you keep coming up with ideas for great new products?" The answer is simple: because I couldn't, and wouldn't, do anything else.

In 2009, I attended a meeting with the Senior VP of product development at my company. The meeting was in the New York City offices of Givaudan, the world's largest flavor and fragrance house. We were there to talk about a new fragrance for Iman.

Early in the meeting, a Givaudan executive handed me a small white plastic object and said, "Here, Joy, smell this."

The object was something they used to demonstrate perfume sample scents. It was light and firm and shaped like a raindrop. It looked like a large white pebble, except that it had a depression in the middle of it—like what silly putty would look like if you pressed your thumb into it. I brought the pebble to my nose and smelled it, and I was hit by a lovely, fresh blast of gardenia.

"Wow," is all I said.

The executive took the pebble back, and everyone resumed talking about other fragrances. But all I could think about was that pebble.

I asked him a little more about it. He said it was made of ground-up wood pulp and some other substances that when mixed together formed a plant-based plastic polymer.

"Why is it a plant-based plastic?" I asked.

"Because it holds the scent longer than paper."

"How long?" I asked. "How old is this one?"

"I don't know, maybe two years?" he said.

"And you can smell the scent in the air for that long?"

"Yes."

"And you can put any scent in it?"

"Just about."

"And it can be any shape?"

"Yes, any shape."

"Could you put odor-elimination technology in it, too?"

"I don't see why not," the executive said. "But why would you want to?"

I looked over at my senior VP, and she looked at me. She knew what I was thinking. She *always* knew what I was thinking.

We excused ourselves and went to the ladies' room, and checked under the stalls to make sure no one else was there.

"This is huge, do you understand that?" I whispered.

"Of course I understand that, I've been scribbling notes like crazy!" she said.

We started brainstorming right then and there. What if we mixed a subtle fragrance with an odor-elimination technology and infused it in a polymer that would work to keep your home fresh for two years? And what if, instead of a pebble, we molded little sticks that could go in decorative vases you could put all over the house?

"There's no messy oil so it wouldn't matter if you knocked the jar over," she said.

"Or if the cat knocked it over," I said. "And it's plant-based, so it's safe."

"You could put it next to your baby's crib!"

"You could put it anywhere! And it lasts for two years!"

We took the idea back to HSN—a plant-based polymer that would release a fragrant scent in your home and eliminate odors for over two years! We made beautiful vases with twenty fragrance sticks in each one, and we called it Forever Fragrant.

And after it debuted, it became the first product in the history of HSN to sell more than 100,000 units in a single day, breaking the network's all-time record.

One night at my house, I just couldn't find my reading glasses. I looked everywhere, and I finally gave up. So instead of reading, I sat down and started thinking about glasses.

There were a couple of problems with them, as I saw it, besides not remembering where you put them. If you bought the cheap drugstore kind, they were usually poorly made and tended to fall apart. If you bought expensive frames, they inevitably got sat on or smushed or hopelessly bent. And then those little rubber nose pieces always dug into your skin.

My Senior VP and I did some research and, sure enough, we discovered the industry markup on most frames and glasses is enormous. In other words, quality glasses weren't that expensive for factories to make, but they were very expensive for customers to buy.

That gave me another idea.

What if I could make quality reading glasses for a price that was so low, we could sell more than one pair at a time? Then, you could put them down anywhere, and you'd always find a pair somewhere.

We got down to work. We added spring hinges so the frames would be comfortable and also not break. We redesigned the shape of the bridge so it didn't pinch your nose. We made the frames lightweight and we designed them in an array of beautiful styles and colors. Best of all, we figured out how to offer not one, not two, not even three, but *ten* reading glasses for what people usually paid for just one.

Our Shades Readers were another smash hit at HSN, and to date we've sold more than 13 million pairs. Oprah even chose them as one of her holiday picks. They were successful because of one thing:

We didn't sell reading glasses the way companies wanted to sell them.

We sold them the way people wanted to buy them.

A few years ago, my Senior VP and I visited a company in North Carolina called Edison Nation. It's a company that raises funds to help inventors produce, license, and sell their creations. They'd been wanting to work with HSN for some time, and we agreed to fly down and take a look at some of the products they were developing.

One by one, the products came out. They were all clever, but nothing was really striking us as something that would really improve our customer's lives. The meeting wound down, and we got up to leave.

But as I was walking out, I noticed a strange white object on a shelf. It looked like a slice of PVC piping with a peg through the middle, and a golf ball spinning on the peg.

"What is this?" I asked the engineer.

"I don't know," he said.

I held it for a while. I turned it over in my hands. And then I saw it.

Luggage wheels.

Ordinary wheels are attached to a fixed axle, but this device was a ball that could rotate inside the tube, which gave it a lot more flexibility of movement. That's what made me realize its potential.

From having traveled so much, I knew that 97 percent of all luggage damage happens when the wheels break. How many times have you seen people dragging their luggage behind them because a wheel fell off? Exactly.

Flying back home from North Carolina that night, we envisioned a new approach to luggage. Our bags wouldn't have four bulky wheels, but rather four of these sleek new spinning-ball wheels.

And besides being more stable, the wheels would also have a low profile, which meant our bags could have more space for clothing without getting any taller.

"Can you imagine getting all that packing space back?" I said to my Senior VP.

"And the lower profile would mean wheels would never break off," she said.

It took a short plane ride to come up with the idea. But to make the actual luggage?

That took us *three years*.

There were a million details to deal with. Fracture points. Spin ratios. Ball bearing types. Drop tests. We had to make twenty-three different 3D-printed prototypes for the wheels before we got them right.

But in the end, our Joy Luggage with patented SpinBall technology became another phenomenon at HSN.

I guess you could say that, in a way, we reinvented the wheel.

The dictionary defines success as "the accomplishment of an aim or purpose." But how do *you* define it? How do you define "getting there"? What is your aim and purpose in life?

We all get to define success in different ways.

But sometimes, we don't define it at all.

Instead, we settle for someone else's definition of success. Or we chase goals that were never really ours in the first place. Or we do what other people expect of us, rather than what we expect of ourselves.

That's why it's absolutely critical for us to sit down and do the hard work of defining what success truly means to us.

Let's say an accountant makes a really great living, has the most important clients, and earns the respect of everyone in his field. By all objective measures, the accountant is a success.

But what if the accountant's real and true dream is to open a small surf shop by a beach somewhere?

And what if the accountant quits his job, moves his family to the coast, and finally fulfills his dream by opening his tiny surf shop?

And what if the surf shop only brings in a fraction of what the accountant used to make in his old job?

Is the accountant still a success?

Well, if the accountant is genuinely inspired and energized for the first time ever, and if the accountant's family absolutely loves waking up to sunshine every day and spending their afternoons surfing and eating seafood, and if the accountant's little surf shop brings comfort and beauty and happiness to the people who shop there—then, to me, the (now former) accountant is a *huge* success.

My definition of success is simple: it means getting to do what you love to do. In that sense, I had success while I was making the Miracle Mop in the back of the auto body shop. I had success at my first office in Deer Park, and at the next one in Edgewood. As long as I kept doing what I loved, I was successful.

And when, over the years, I was told time and time again that I should care about other things, or define success in some other way, I held on tight to my own definition. I fought to stay true to it.

People would say, "Joy, you could make more money if you do this or that," but that was never my goal—my goal was to make great, innovative products that people really needed, not products with extra features that could sell for higher prices.

It didn't matter what the world thought I should be doing. It didn't matter that some people define success in terms of fame and wealth. What mattered was *my* definition of success, not anyone else's.

Because when you *define* your own success—and your own joy—then you can begin to *design* it.

I need to clarify one thing. I said that my definition of success is doing what I love to do, and that's true, but that's not the whole definition. There is more to it.

My definition of success—or, I should say, my definition of a truly joyful life—is doing what I love to do *with the people I love most*.

Which is why I should have mentioned that the senior VP I referred to earlier is named Christie.

As in, my *daughter* Christie.

# 42

Christie was always an overachiever, just like me.

She was president of her class, captain of the cheerleading squad, and the commencement speaker at graduation.

On top of that, Christie was one of the most kind, caring, open-hearted people I'd ever known. From when she was young, Christie was always the mama bear, looking out for everyone and making sure we were all all right—even me.

Growing up, Christie wanted to become a wedding planner. After graduating from Providence College in Rhode Island, she landed a great job at Coburn Communications, a major public relations agency in New York City. She worked hard, made great contacts, and impressed everyone. She was on her way.

But Christie grew up in the product business with me. She was by my side for just about everything I went through. She thought the same way

I did, and sometimes we didn't even need to talk to know we agreed on something—we just looked at each other and we knew.

So when she got older, I asked her what she thought about coming to work with me (a mother can dream, can't she?).

I never, ever pressured Christie to do anything, or tried to steer her in any direction. And I understood she had her own dreams and plans. But I just had to ask. I knew Christie would be an enormous asset to any company she worked for. I guess I just wanted that company to be mine.

And Christie said yes!

Christie left her job at Coburn and came to work at HSN. Her first years at the company were wonderful for both of us. She was right there in the trenches with me, growing and fighting and learning. Seeing her happy and thriving like that was everything a mother could ever wish for.

It was around then that Christie came to me one day—as a daughter, not a colleague—and told me she'd met someone.

He was an incredibly handsome, charismatic chef—the kind of man who inspired awe in everyone around him. He was born in Europe, spoke four languages, and trained with the best French masters. We were all dazzled by him, and clearly Christie was, too.

At first they dated long-distance, but soon he moved to New York and proposed to Christie. The wedding was like a fairy tale—it was in a castle on Long Island, with Bobby as the best man and Jackie as the maid of honor. Everything seemed just perfect.

But it wasn't.

Within a month of getting married, we learned things about him that were shocking. About his past and his personality and who he was and how he treated people. It was like someone flipped a switch, and he became a different person. It was like a terrible nightmare.

Christie, the bighearted protector of everyone, had her life shattered by someone she trusted with her heart.

She tried extremely hard to fix things, but in the end she made the painful decision to get a divorce. She moved in with me, and in the mornings we'd drive to work together, and at night we'd sit on my bed and talk and cry, and then we'd get up and go to work again. Seeing her feel so lost and distraught was excruciating, and it made me feel so helpless, but all I could do was be there for her when she needed me.

Perhaps as a way to cope with everything, Christie poured herself into her job at HSN. I watched her work harder and longer than anyone could ever expect. She got there early, stayed late, and involved herself in everything. It was like she was willing herself back to strength, so that she could become the person she was meant to be.

Christie emerged as a force at HSN. Exceptionally smart, quick on her feet, endlessly resourceful. She just kept growing and reaching new heights, and she pushed me to reach new heights, too. She pulled herself out of the darkest place she'd ever been in, and transformed into a true powerhouse.

But wait—there's more. About a year after Christie's divorce, she attended a birthday party I organized for one of my co-hosts and good friends at HSN, Shannon Smith. There were a lot of people from work there, including an HSN producer named Matt.

Matt had been at HSN since I arrived there. He was smart and handsome and talented, and I had worked directly with him as my producer for years. Matt and Christie worked together a lot, too, but for some reason they just never connected.

Then, at the party, Matt and Christie happened to wander into the same cluster of people who were talking and laughing in my living room. I was nearby and I wandered into the group, too.

"So Matt, when is your birthday?" I asked.

He looked at me a little funny.

"May 19," he said.

"Oh, really? That's Christie's birthday, too!" I said, my face a picture of complete surprise (yeah, right) at the coincidence (ha!).

Matt and Christie laughed, and they wound up talking until the party was over.

And then, lo and behold, they fell in love.

Matt proposed to Christie on Christmas Eve, and they got married in a small ceremony in Napa Valley, on a balcony overlooking the lush hills and the valley. It was magical. After everything that happened, I thought I'd never see Christie that happy again.

Earlier, I wrote that we shouldn't wait around for Prince Charming. By that, I meant that the task of rescuing ourselves is ours and ours alone. Look at Christie. She rescued herself, and she built herself back up, and she reinvented who she was. She created her own brave and joyful life.

And then, because life is funny sometimes, her Prince Charming came along anyway.

# 43

What about Bobby?

Growing up, Bobby was the only boy in a house full of women. On some weekends, us girls would go to the mall to do some shopping, and Bobby would have to come along. But he never complained. Instead, he'd find a place to sit, pull out a book, and read until we were ready to go. Bobby read voraciously. On vacations, he'd read two books in a day—and a dozen in a week—with no problem at all.

And so, almost by fate, Bobby became an incredibly sharp and lively thinker, with an ability to absorb and process information that seemed almost effortless (I know, I'm bragging, but come on, I'm his mom).

Bobby also grew up without his father around every day. And so he was the person we asked to fix things around the house. If the TV broke, or the clocks needed resetting, or the printer was jammed, we asked Bobby to fix it. And he did. And in the process, he developed this innate belief that, if he looked at a problem with enough patience and attention, he could fix it.

Bobby was most inspired by my lawyer, Tony Curto, and how Tony was the one person I leaned on during the major moments in my life—how Tony was my Answer Man. That was how Bobby found his calling in life—he decided he was going to be an attorney, just like Tony, and he was going to help people with their biggest problems, problems that seemed to have no solution, just like Tony had done for me.

So Bobby went to Georgetown University, and after that to Columbia Law School, and after that he was hired by Cravath, Swaine & Moore, one of the most prestigious law firms in the country. Before long, Bobby was running massive litigations for major clients (I know, I know, I'll stop).

The best part was that I could see how much Bobby loved what he was doing. I mean, he absolutely loved it. He worked unbelievable hours, 120 hours a week, but because he was doing what he'd been preparing for all his life—providing answers and fixing things—it seemed he would have worked even longer if he'd found a way to add an extra hour or two to each day.

In fact, most years Bobby only took one short vacation from work. One of those vacations was to New Orleans, where he joined some college roommates for a bachelor party. It just so happened that while he was there, one of his friends ran into a woman he knew from back in New York. Her name was Theo, and she was a beautiful aspiring actress from England. She joined Bobby and his group, and later that evening her handbag was stolen. With no cell phone, she couldn't call back to England for help.

So Bobby lent her his work cell phone, which had an international plan. That's how Bobby wound up with her phone number.

And wouldn't you know—back in New York, Bobby and Theo went on a date, sharing a breakfast of fresh fruit on a bench in Washington Square Park. Three years later, Bobby took her to the very same bench, got down on one knee, and proposed. Theo said yes, and they were married in a beautiful ceremony in Hawaii.

And all because he couldn't even take a short vacation without bringing his work phone.

While Bobby was building his career at Cravath, my business was growing quickly. That was a great thing, but it also meant that Christie and I and a lot of other people had to work long hours almost every weekend. I needed to find talented people I could hire, and fast.

I hadn't allowed myself to imagine Bobby coming to work with me. I knew that he loved his work at Cravath—I mean, he really *loved* it. Six years into the job, Bobby was carving his own path—and there was no way I was ever going to get him to come work with me.

But that didn't mean I couldn't *ask*.

"So what about coming to work with me?" I said one night when Bobby was over at my house.

"I'm sorry, I can't," Bobby said.

He said the same thing when I asked him the next time.

And the time after that.

But on one night after I asked him, Bobby went home and talked it over with Theo.

"I feel like I'm already doing what I was born to do," he said. "What do you think I should do?"

"If you don't do it, you might regret it for the rest of your life," Theo said. "You said you want to help people who need you? Well, Joy needs you."

Bobby knew she was right.

And so he surprised a *lot* of people by leaving one of the best law firms in the world, and coming to work with me, too.

When Bobby joined Christie and me, we were able to fly even higher. Bobby threw himself into every facet of the business and he approached every endeavor with ferocious intelligence (I know, I said I'd stop bragging, so sue me). With Bobby on board, we redesigned the brand, launched incredible marketing campaigns, got started on social media, built a new website, restructured the organization, opened new warehouses, implemented an amazing cloud-based warehouse-management system, and attracted major new customers.

Oh yeah, and there's one other thing Bobby did when he arrived.

Bobby became my Answer Man.

# 44

And finally we get to my younger daughter, my baby—Jackie.

When Jackie was little, she was uncommonly fashion-conscious. She couldn't go to sleep at night until she'd spent a lot of time picking out a perfectly color-coordinated outfit and laying it out for herself to wear in the morning.

So I shouldn't have really been surprised when, one day when she was in high school, Jackie told me she wanted to be a model.

Now, Jackie is truly beautiful, and I'm not just saying that because I'm her mother. She is tall and she has gorgeous blond hair and a dazzling smile. But modeling can be a brutal industry, and I just didn't see that as the path for her in her life.

But you know how I said we have to carve our own paths through life, no matter who tries to stop us?

Well, Jackie took that lesson to heart.

She didn't let anyone stop her.

Not even when the "anyone" was me.

For instance, when she decided to go into Manhattan to meet with a modeling agent, she didn't ask me to drive her. She didn't even tell me she was going. Instead, she called her father, Tony, and he drove her in.

After high school, Jackie enrolled at the Fashion Institute of Technology in New York City, and got straight As. But she left early to devote herself full-time to modeling. That wasn't an easy time for her; there were long dry spells and lots of rejections, which made me very worried for her. I worried if she was eating right, and I worried about her going to auditions, and basically I worried about everything.

But Jackie just kept pushing forward.

And over time I could see she was winning victories along the way. She was signed by a talent agent, then chosen as a fit model for designer Vivienne Tam. She worked a small fashion show in Manhattan, then moved to Greece to work in Europe. She was photographed for the cover of a magazine.

Then came her biggest break, when she was chosen to be one of the models of the hit TV show *Project Runway*. In fact, she became *the* standout model on the show. After that, Jackie just blossomed. She hosted an Internet show called *AfterBuzz*, and she became a fashion and style expert for several different outlets, including VH1, *Lucky* magazine, *The Wendy Williams Show*, *The View*, and *Extra*. She also hosted *Us Weekly*'s fashion report, "Red Carpet Daily."

Thank goodness she didn't listen to me.

Even when it came to dating, Jackie did things her way. One night, one of her boyfriends pulled up to the house in a big van with curtains covering its windows. He was a muscular wrestler/football-player-type, and through the kitchen window I watched him jump out of the van and strut toward the house. I turned to Jackie and said just one word.

"No."

Turns out I was wrong about that, too.

Jackie and Sean—a smart, funny, handsome, All-State wrestler—have been together now for fifteen years, and no couple I know is more connected and devoted to each other. They're not in any rush to get married, mainly because they're both so busy—Jackie with her fashion and TV work, and Sean as a teacher and coach of a wrestling program for inner-city children he started in New York City.

But really, they're the most married couple I know.

Not too long ago, Jackie called me and said, "Hey, Mom, did you have someone at HSN call me?"

"No," I said. "Why, who called?"

"Jen, the talent executive. They asked me to be a style expert on HSN."

It was true. Jen had seen Jackie on VH1 and thought she'd be a perfect fit for HSN. Jen didn't consult me about it, and I had nothing to do with the call. Jackie and I talked it over, and Jackie agreed to appear on HSN as a red-carpet reporter and a style expert. I remember watching her first appearance on the network, and marveling at how incredibly self-assured she was. She was so bright and so vibrant and impossible not to be charmed by, and she brought an entirely new dimension to what we were doing on the air.

In the end, Jackie didn't come to HSN.

HSN came to her.

And, just like that, the Core Four were back together again.

Christie, Bobby, and Jackie were there with me every step of the way. In hotel rooms, waiting for me as I fought some battle somewhere. In the auto body shop, helping me make Miracle Mops. In the warehouse, assembling Rolykits. Everywhere I went, they went with me. They were my rock, and I was theirs.

My children embody so many of the lessons and insights in this book. They never stopped discovering themselves. They didn't take no for an answer. They didn't listen to experts (even when the expert was me!). Most fortunately for me, they leaned on each other, and on me, and they saw the chance to work with their family as a blessing.

That's why my definition of a joyful life is doing what I love to do with the people I love most.

Because, to me, my children are the true wealth and treasure of my life.

# 45

In 2006, I met a producer named Ken Mok while filming a TV show in Los Angeles. He asked if he could take me to dinner before I flew back to New York, and we agreed to meet in a Chinese restaurant across the street from my hotel.

Over dinner, Ken got me to tell him my life story. The marriage, the mop, QVC, HSN, all of it. The whole crazy trajectory of my journey. Ken was hearing most of it for the first time, and he asked lots of questions and bubbled with enthusiasm. I didn't know why he was so interested.

After dinner Ken paid the check and we hugged goodbye.

"Joy," he said, "one day, I am going to write a movie about your life."

"Ken, you're so cute," I said. "Goodbye."

I'd hear from Ken a couple of times a year, through phone calls and emails. He'd tell me that he was just checking in, and he'd promise me again that he was going to make a movie about my life. I'd always laugh and wish him luck. Not once did I take him seriously.

Several years passed. I got another call from Ken, and this time he said he was in an office with two big Hollywood producers.

"We're going to write your movie!" Ken said.

"Great!" I said (trying to sound like I actually believed such a thing could happen—a movie about me).

And then I went back to work.

Well, Ken didn't give up.

He sat down and he wrote a script, and eventually I learned the actress Sandra Bullock was interested in it. So was Fox, the movie studio. Then the actress Kristen Wiig was mentioned. Finally, some more papers were signed, and Ken called me and said, "David wants to do the movie, and he wants Jennifer to play you."

David?

Jennifer?

Who?

The David was David O. Russell, one of Hollywood's most inventive and successful directors, and the man behind the hit movie *Silver Linings Playbook*.

And the Jennifer was Jennifer Lawrence, who won a Best Actress Oscar for *Silver Linings Playbook* and is one of the most brilliant young actresses in all of Hollywood.

Oh, and I also learned the movie would star Robert De Niro and Bradley Cooper, too.

That's when I started to really pay attention.

David started calling me to learn more about me, and I'd get calls from him at nine in the morning and six in the evening and 3:00 a.m. Sometimes we'd end up talking for hours. Honestly, we must have spent a couple of hundred hours talking about my journey (which was the best free therapy anyone could ever ask for).

At first, the whole notion of a movie about my life made me skeptical. But the more I thought about the movie, the more I fell in love with the idea. You see, everyone has a story to tell, and this movie would tell mine. And if my story resonated with a lot of people, and maybe even motivated them to take action, then that would definitely be a good thing.

David called the movie *JOY*, and it premiered at the storied Ziegfeld Theatre in New York City. I was a little nervous about going to the premiere, to be honest. Despite all the hours I spend on TV, I haven't had fame rearrange my life all that much. I'm perfectly okay skipping the big ball.

But my children were all so excited to be going, and that was more than enough to get me excited, too. Jackie helped me pick out a dress, and she and Christie and Theo all wore long, beautiful gowns. Bobby, Matt, and Sean put on elegant black suits. Looking at all of them that day, I felt so much love and pride.

I wished that I could have frozen the moment in time.

We got into two cars and drove to the theater in Manhattan. When we pulled up to the entrance, just before we got out, Jackie grabbed me by the arm.

"Brace yourself," she said.

"For what?" I asked.

Then I stepped out of the car, and flashbulbs exploded.

"That's Joy," I heard people yelling. "That's the real Joy!"

Christie took me by one arm and Bobby by the other, and we walked the red carpet through a crush of fans and photographers. It was only about a hundred-foot walk, but it probably took us half an hour. We'd walk three steps, then stop for another round of smiles and photos and well-wishes.

Then I heard someone say, "Joy, get over here!" and I looked up and it was Jennifer Lawrence, and I went over and got between her and Bradley Cooper as more flashbulbs went off.

And as I stood there, I couldn't get over the feeling that I was on the outside of everything that was happening, looking in. As if I was watching from the sidelines as someone else posed for photos next to Jennifer and Bradley.

My mind just couldn't catch up to what was happening.

I can easily close my eyes and summon the bedroom I had as a little girl. I can see my old twin bed, and my dresser, and in the corner the little wooden desk where I sat for hundreds and hundreds of hours making my creations. It's where I kept all my pencils and paper and crayons and made all my own greeting cards, and it's where I'd take articles of clothing my mother bought me and cut off the sleeves or shorten them or otherwise change them because I believed I could make them better.

When I sat at the little wooden desk in the corner, I entered a world where anything was possible, and where everything I could ever dream up could become reality.

But the one thing I never, ever dreamed, not in all the time I lived in my magical, limitless world, was that one day I'd be attending the star-studded premiere of a big Hollywood movie, let alone a movie about *me*.

As far-reaching as my imagination might have been, the reality of my life wound up exceeding it.

The movie *JOY* proved to me that as long as we stay open to new paths and new adventures, and as long as we keep working hard, no goal is out of reach for us, no matter how lofty our dreams may be. I mean, if they could make a movie about me, skinny little Joy from Long Island, then *anything* is possible.

But despite all the success and opportunity that has come my way, I always try to remember one really important thing.

No matter how successful we may become, we need to stay as grounded in our lives as we possibly can.

We need to stay *in* our lives, not above them.

Success doesn't mean we magically float to a place that is different from our lives. And it doesn't mean that we become different people. There is no such thing as being too successful or too famous to stay close to the people we love and continue to pay attention to the smallest details of our lives.

The Joy who was on the red carpet that night was the same Joy who mopped a small square of flooring four hundred times in one day at a Michigan Kmart, and walked out with blisters and borrowed slippers.

The same Joy who for years bought her children Christmas presents on sale, and drove a beat-up Lumina minivan for way too long.

The same Joy who calls her children six times a day, every day, and who keeps a massive group text going with them for weeks at a time.

The same Joy who can still use a tape gun to seal up a package as fast as any UPS worker out there (if you don't believe me, just watch me do it sometime).

So even in that impossibly surreal moment on the red carpet at the Ziegfeld, standing between Jennifer and Bradley and about to go in and watch a movie about my life, I forced myself to remember who I was, and remember where I came from.

That night, my daughter Jackie wasn't just my guest at the movie premiere. She was also working the red carpet as an on-air style reporter for her *Us Weekly* show, "Red Carpet Daily."

That night, it just so happened that Jackie's job was to interview . . . me.

Jackie was tough and independent, and she'd carved her own path through life, and she'd taken her own hard journey, and now that journey had brought her here, to a theater in Manhattan for a big movie premiere.

And I was tough and independent, too, and I had carved my own path, and I'd taken my own hard journey, and now my journey had brought me to the very same place at the very same time.

And so there we were, a mother and a daughter, sharing a truly magical moment together, on a red carpet, in designer gowns, with flashbulbs exploding, about to see a movie called *JOY*.

It was like my life had come full circle in the most beautiful way.

Jackie was standing there, microphone in hand.

"Okay, so Mom, tell us what it's like to be at the premiere of a movie about your own life?" Jackie asked me as the camera rolled.

I can't even remember what my answer was.

But I do know what I wanted to say.

I wanted to say, "Jackie, I am the luckiest mom in the world."

# 46

I was in the delivery room with Christie, who was about to give birth to her first child. Matt was there, and Jackie, too, while Bobby and Sean were in the waiting room. Theo was on FaceTime from a TV set in New York. And Christie's father Tony—who still hates hospitals but also hates missing any big family event—he was there, too, shuffling back and forth between the delivery and waiting rooms.

We all stayed with Christie at the hospital through the night and into the morning, until it was time. The doctor rushed in, and the nurse began to clear the room of any extra people. One of the extra people was Tony, and the nurse asked him to leave. A few moments later, I looked around the delivery room and Tony was gone. Then the doctor got ready to deliver Christie's baby.

Suddenly, the nurse stopped him.

"Um, there's still an extra person in the room," she said.

"I don't care, we have to go now," the doctor responded.

I looked around the room, wondering what the nurse meant.

Then I saw them.

Tony's white loafers sticking out from behind the long window curtains.

Tony doesn't like to miss out on anything. But Tony also can't stand the sight of blood. So Tony hid behind the curtains—just like he stayed plastered to the wall on the day I gave birth to Christie nearly thirty years earlier—while Christie brought our first grandchild into the world.

His name was Christopher, and he was just the most darling, perfect, beautiful little baby ever. He weighed a whopping ten pounds.

"You just gave birth to a baby deer," Jackie told her.

When Jackie handed Christopher to me in the delivery room, I felt an incredible burst of pure and powerful love. It was one of the happiest moments of my life.

Meanwhile, Tony was still hiding behind the curtains. He had to make sure every bit of blood had been cleaned up before he could come out.

In 2017, Christie and Matt had a second beautiful, precious child, Alexandria. And you know what?

Tony hid behind the curtains that time, too.

If my story is about anything, it's about family.

I haven't been very lucky in the romance department. Several years after my split from Tony, I got married again, but that relationship didn't work out. Maybe my luck will change in the future, but even if it doesn't, that's okay.

It's okay because I've been blessed with a family that I love more than words can ever convey. I always talk about my three children, but really I have six children: Christie and Matt, Bobby and Theo, and Jackie and Sean. They are the reason I try to live the way I do—bravely, justly, creatively.

My story is also about the American Dream, which has everything to do with family, too.

America is a young nation. Most of us are only three or four generations away from the people who sailed across oceans to start their new lives here, and some of us even fewer. Some of us have parents and grandparents who followed their hopes and dreams to this country.

And all of those dreamers who made that dangerous trip—*they were all inventors.*

They were brave and creative and determined and hardworking, and they invented themselves and invented their lives in a new place called America.

And that bravery and creativity and determination was passed on to the next generation, and then to the next, and our great-grandparents infused their children with this wonderful mind-set, and those children infused their children, and on and on.

And now this beautiful spark of invention and innovation exists in the very soul of the country, and in the souls of every one of us.

We might not have made the perilous journey on a boat, like some of those who came before us. But we reflect the same passionate, driving force that made them risk everything for a chance to re-create themselves.

That force lives inside us all. It's part of our inheritance. Part of our wiring. Part of what makes us who we are. If we have the courage to summon it, it will empower us to invent our best and brightest selves.

Now, I know as well as anyone that taking the first step in any meaningful pursuit can be scary and intimidating. Believe me, I've been there. Getting started can be the hardest part of the journey—that's when the fear and doubt and uncertainty are at their height. I understand that kind of self-doubt. Sometimes I still have to fight it.

But I have learned how to push through those feelings, and how to tap into the brave and creative part of myself. How to tap into the great inventor that lives inside us all.

The life we create for ourselves is the ultimate product. And we have the power to make it our best work.

More than anything, I want for you to embrace this power and enjoy a new romance with your life.

To open your mind and get rid of boundaries and explore new paths.

To connect with your creativity and discover your strengths and become your very best self.

Because when we live a truly joyful life, we get to share our unique and beautiful light with the world.

A great adventure awaits us.

All we have to do is take the first step.

# THE
# BLUEPRINT

I've been told that a lot of my core principles and beliefs are counter-intuitive—that they go against the conventional way of thinking in the world of business.

And I'm okay with that.

You see, the insights in this book didn't come from seminars or an executive training program. I learned them by doing things I probably had no business doing, and making real mistakes in real life, and by figuring out how to do it better the next time around.

Almost every lesson in my life began as a hardship or setback—a broken marriage, a disastrous deal, an impossible deadline.

And the lessons themselves emerged out of how I handled those hardships and setbacks.

In other words, I didn't just learn these lessons.

I *earned* these lessons.

I wrote this book because I wanted to share all the things I've learned on my journey, in the hope that my beliefs might help and inspire and motivate you on yours.

*Any single one of them,* on its own, can create a meaningful change in the way you look at the world, and the way you look at your life.

Taken together, I believe they can guide you through a life that is free of unnecessary obstacles and full of authentic, creative moments.

A life in which you find success on *your* terms.

A more joyful life.

People always stop me and ask, "Joy, what's your secret?"

Well, here it is.

## EVERYTHING IS A PRODUCT

I've heard people say, "Oh, Joy has some kind of superpower, that's why she's so successful." It's flattering, but it's not true. I have the same power we all have:

The power to make our lives work better.

Sometimes we forget we have the power—and the right—to have an opinion about our own lives. If things aren't going well, we could shrug and say, "Oh well, what can I do about it, that's life." But we should never do that, because we *always* have a say in how our life unfolds.

There's a little trick we can use to remind ourselves that our voice matters.

Think of everything in your life as a product.

Your house, your job, your relationships, everything. Think of them as products. Then think of yourself as the consumer of those products. *As the consumer, you are entitled to decide whether or not each product in your life works to your satisfaction.* If it does, great!

But if it doesn't, you have the right—and the power—to fix it.

## TUNE IN WITH EMPATHY

We all have the ability to understand and share the emotions of others—it's called empathy.

*To be truly successful in life, we need to turn on this power and seek out a loving and caring approach to everyone in our path.*

One of the reasons I've been successful as an inventor is because I care so deeply and so passionately about the people I make products for. My connection to the consumer is direct and authentic because *I am the consumer myself*.

When I'm creating a new product, the *only* thing that matters is its value to consumers, and whether or not it will meaningfully improve their lives. That's what drives every decision I make and every turn I take.

To accomplish anything meaningful, we need to understand the value of what we're doing, not just for ourselves, but for the other people in our lives. Everything we do, everything we create, everything we put out into the world, is a product, and we must care deeply and passionately about how that product improves the lives of those around us.

So turn on this power, and tune in to the people you serve. Make their perspective your perspective. If you do this in all aspects of your life, success will always follow.

## YOU DON'T HAVE TO BE
## GOOD TO GET STARTED

Some people think that in order to create something meaningful in any field, you have to already understand that field. To start anything great, they say, you have got to know exactly what you're doing.

*But you don't. You don't have to be good to get started. You just need to dive in and get going.*

When we're young we don't have these barriers. We don't worry about being good or messing up. I didn't know anything about appliances when I tried to reinvent my family's toaster oven when I was young. It didn't work, but you know what? I learned something, and I wasn't afraid to keep trying new things.

But as we grow older, we tend to shut our fearlessness off. We are taught that being skeptical is smart and we become our own worst critic. We allow our fear of not succeeding to stop us from even trying in the first place. And that's the real mistake.

Look at me. Being far outside of the home goods industry didn't stop me from creating the Miracle Mop. If I'd followed the rules, I'd never even have gotten off the ground.

It's only by getting started—by taking the first step—that we'll ever make any progress. It's okay to make mistakes and mess things up along the way—that's how we learn what works and what doesn't. The only real mistake is not having the courage to get started.

## NEVER STOP DISCOVERING YOURSELF

Our paths through life will *always* change, whether we want them to or not. And you know what? That's not a bad thing, it's a *great* thing.

I believe life is a series of amazing discoveries about ourselves, and the only way we can make those discoveries is by staying open to new paths and new adventures.

I call it shifting our skis. When I was younger, I skied down mountains at 50 mph. I didn't have the luxury of seeing the whole path down the mountain. I just had to get started and see where the mountain took me. And when I saw a tree blocking my path, I shifted my skis and set out on a new path.

That applies to my life, too. When new paths presented themselves, I was never afraid to take them. I've tried to always be ready to shift my skis. And it's served me well.

Be careful. Don't listen to the inner voice that chose your path twenty years ago. Listen to the voice that is talking to you *right now. In business, and in life, we need to stay ready to explore new paths with as much courage as we can muster.*

And when we do, we will discover amazing new things about ourselves, and about how strong and capable and courageous and powerful we can be.

## ONCE IT'S IN THE AIR, ACT

I've learned that opportunities are very, very fleeting. They are windows that stay open for only a very short time, and you're never sure when they'll slam shut.

*One of the keys to being successful in any endeavor is taking action as soon as possible.*

Think about my idea for a fluorescent flea collar. Everyone told me it was a great idea, but I got distracted and put it on the back burner, and someone beat me to the invention. The opportunity was gone forever.

And that also applies to families. How many times have you said to your children, "Let's go do this," and then time passes and excuses get made and everyone goes off and does their own thing?

Here's how I look at it now: the minute we have a great idea for anything, some clock out there in the universe starts ticking. Once we commit to that idea, we have to get started immediately, or else we'll only allow more and more things to get in our way. A great idea is only great if we act on it quickly and decisively.

So be decisive, be brave, and get started on your great idea *right now*. Because once it's in the air, the race is on.

## EVERYTHING HAPPENS FOR A REASON

I believe that everything happens for a reason. Every twist, every turn, pushes us closer to the place we're really meant to be.

When I was at Pace University, and I skipped a quiz to go to the pub with a girl I hardly knew, I was following some strange instinct I didn't even understand. My comfortable routine was shattered.

But because I followed that instinct, I made new friends, met my future husband, and saw my life change dramatically—and for the better.

Sometimes we need to listen to our most powerful instincts and let them lead us where they will—even if it's out of our comfort zone. We shouldn't be afraid to try something totally out of character, especially if we feel that life is pulling us in that direction.

Unexpected twists and turns and even outright failures can be very frightening, but they can also be transformative. *Staying open to the idea that everything happens for a reason empowers us to become who we're really meant to be—because anything that happens, good or bad, is ultimately part of our journey to success.*

## THERE IS NO PATH, CARVE YOUR OWN

Just because something has never been done before, doesn't mean it can't be done. If your idea is something new and different, you probably won't find a well-worn path that leads to its creation. But that's okay. That's how a creative life works.

You've got to carve your own path.

Sometimes, we can get boxed in by what's expected of us. My mother Toots, for instance, grew up in a tradition that called for her to get married, have children, and tend to her family. And Tony's father Joe was expected to follow in the family tradition and become a banker. His life was totally laid out for him.

But after my parents separated, my mother carved a brand-new path for herself, as a working woman. And my father-in-law Joe never became a banker—he carved his own path in the field of the arts and lived his own definition of success.

Trying something new and daring in our lives can lead us to feel unstable and a little out at sea—but that's okay. We need to embrace that feeling because it is proof that we're growing and fighting and dreaming and daring to follow a path of our own.

As an inventor, I've never believed that just because something doesn't exist, it can't. And I'm not just talking about inventing products. I'm talking about inventing our *lives*. There is no set path for any of us. We can break with tradition, try new challenges, and see where that takes us. *Because the key to a joyful life is not following the path that's been traveled a million times before. The key is carving our own path.*

## YOU DON'T HAVE TO DO IT ALL

Sometimes we feel like we have to be the box-checkers of our lives. We make a list, and we don't stop until we check off every box. We strive for perfection. But none of us are perfect, and none of us need to be. Perfection is exhausting, and it shouldn't be our goal, anyway.

When I had my three children in four years, I tried really hard to check off every box and be the perfect mother. But in the end I tried to do too much, and I learned I couldn't do it all.

And when I was working on the Miracle Mop, I couldn't always make it to every one of Bobby's hockey games or Christie's recitals or Jackie's bake sales, and I felt bad about it. But that was okay, too.

It's okay to not check every box, or cross off every to-do, and it's okay to feel bad about it. But don't let it stop your momentum. We're going to miss some important moments along the way, guaranteed, so let's try not to beat ourselves up.

When I'm at home, I *am* a box-checker. If I see a pillow that's smushed, I un-smush it right away. But our family relationships and businesses will *never* be as neat and orderly as our houses (if you're like me and you're a hopeless un-smusher).

*So when things get tough and doing it all seems impossible, remember—I didn't do it all, and neither should you.*

## DON'T WAIT FOR PRINCE CHARMING

When I was young I fully believed that Prince Charming would come and rescue me one day. I'm guessing a lot of us did. But then I went through a difficult divorce, and that was the end of my cherished belief that my life, my husband, my family, would always be perfect and ideal.

I came to realize that no one was going to come along and "rescue" me. The only person who could rescue me was me. The responsibility for making my life work better was mine and mine alone.

I'm not saying there weren't a lot of people who helped me get through difficult times, because there were. Even my ex-husband Tony played a part in his own way. But ultimately, the responsibility of creating the life I wanted for myself fell solely on me.

Maybe Prince Charmings do exist, and maybe they're on the way. For some, maybe they're already here.

But we don't need to wait around to be rescued. In life, we're going to find love in lots of different, beautiful, wonderful, unexpected places and ways. Love waits for us everywhere. *But creating the lives we want, and fixing what might be broken, is something we all have the power to do ourselves.*

We get to be the ones who do the rescuing.

## LOOK FOR THE LIGHT, BRIGHT PEOPLE

I've learned that we are only as capable as the people around us believe us to be. If we're surrounded by people who are negative and unsupportive, they can drag us down—while people who are positive and supportive and enthusiastic provide the oxygen for our flame.

One of the big keys in gaining momentum in work and in life is surrounding ourselves with light, bright people.

Meeting Ronni through the PTA of my children's school opened my eyes to how important it is to be around light, bright people. Ronni had so much positive, nourishing energy, and she emboldened me to reach higher than I would have on my own. And I did the same for her. Together, we accomplished amazing things, more than we could have ever dreamed.

In life, we have every right to choose to be around people who believe in us and support us and make us feel better and stronger. We must be vigilant about the people we allow to play a part in our lives. It's one of the most important choices we'll ever make, and leaving it to chance just isn't good enough.

*The people we choose to have in our lives can empower us even beyond our own abilities.* We need to realize that the choice is ours, and we need to choose the light, bright people.

## A LITTLE CAN BE A LOT

There is an instinct in all of us that says an idea needs to be huge and complicated and expensive and earth-shattering in order to be worthy of our time and attention. Like the airplane, or the computer, or the iPhone.

But that's a myth I've spent my whole life disproving.

*An idea doesn't have to be epic in scale to be life-changing. Many times, it is the small, simple, thoughtful ideas that really change our lives.* A simple solution to a simple problem. An incremental improvement. A better way of doing something we do every day.

When I told people I was working on a new kind of mop, nearly everyone said the same thing: *"A mop? Who cares about mops?"* A better mop, they believed, wasn't a big, exciting, epic idea. It just wasn't interesting enough.

But it was to me. I know that even little ideas can make a big, positive, meaningful difference in our lives. Who would have thought a thinner, better hanger would make a difference in people's lives? But after nearly a billion sold, I think it's safe to say that those hangers made a real and meaningful difference in millions and millions of lives, and still do.

In business, and in life, a little can be a lot. And even the simplest, smallest little idea can literally change the world.

## CELEBRATE THE SMALL SUCCESSES

There's a myth in the business world that says we shouldn't stop to celebrate until we cross the finish line. But that just never felt right to me. I believe *no success is too small to celebrate. The journey is too hard and too long for us to deny ourselves little victory celebrations along the way.*

When I was a single mother, just managing to make my children dinner and give them their baths and read them books and put them to sleep with smiling faces was a *major* victory. Organizing a birthday party for thirty kids and thirty sets of parents and having them all go home happy? *Everything* about that achievement was good and right and wonderful. So why not celebrate it!

Whatever the victory, why not give ourselves a high five! Mark the moment and say, *I did it. I orchestrated it. I made it happen.* It may be a tiny moment, but it matters, and it matters a *lot.*

It's human nature to say, *We're not out of the woods yet, let's not get too excited.* But doing anything meaningful will always have hard times built into the process. That's why we need to keep on the lookout for the *good* times—those sweet, wonderful moments when things go right—because they give us the fuel we need to keep going.

## YOU DON'T HAVE TO JUMP OFF A CLIFF

Some people believe that in order to start something new, you have to take drastic actions. Sell your house, take out a million-dollar loan, or otherwise completely upend your life and your family. To start anything worth starting, they believe, you have to jump off a cliff.

But that's not true.

With the Miracle Mop, I started small. Getting started on the idea didn't change my life all that much. I still took my children to school and cooked for them and cleaned up after them and watched TV with them as they fell asleep. But I also took small steps toward my goal. Some of the steps were hard and risky, and, yes, I had to be brave, but none of them were reckless or life-altering.

Believing you have to jump off a cliff is a false impediment. *There are ways to pursue a life of hope and creativity without risking everything.* There are paths to doing it in a way that is sustainable for us and our families. Creativity doesn't have to be all or nothing, and we don't need to do something crazy to get started.

We just need to believe in ourselves, and take the first small step.

## A NO IS NOT A NO

Chances are, if we try to do something daring—something that hasn't been done before—a lot of people will tell us we can't do it. We'll hear *no* a lot.

The buyer for Kmart? He told me *no* when I showed him the Miracle Mop. Not maybe or we'll see, but a flat *no. No, I cannot sell your mop. No one will buy it.*

I'd guess that in my life I've been told *no* a million times. If I put every *no* I've been told in this book, there wouldn't be any room left for anything else.

We need to understand that *no* does not really mean *no. No is not the end of anything. No doesn't shut down all our options—it gives us even more options!*

One option is, How can I change this *no* to a *yes?* Or, Can I go to someone else and get the *yes* I need? Or, What if I just wait a while and try again later? There is *always* a solution to any problem. Even if it looks like a dead end, it never is.

What's more, a *no* is productive! Finding our way around the *no* will make us work harder, be better, think deeper. A *no* gives us the chance to learn something, reset our thinking, and draw motivation—the motivation of proving people wrong.

If we want to create something new and meaningful, people will *always* tell us it can't be done. People will always say *no.* We have to move past these people and find a way to get to a *yes.* We need to realize a *no* is never a *no.*

## TAKE YOUR EYE OFF THE PRIZE

Someone will always tell you, "Never take your eye off the prize. Stay focused on your ultimate goal."

Don't listen to them.

The truth is, when we start any endeavor, we don't really know where we're going to end up. We may think we know, but we don't. We can't. Our paths will change, and our finish line will change, too.

Nearly *all* of my finish lines have changed along the way. It was never my goal to go on live TV and sell Miracle Mops myself. Heck, I still hate public speaking! But when going on live TV became my obvious next step, I poured my heart and soul into it and I made it work.

*Our main focus should be on the very next step we need to take to keep moving forward.* I've learned to be comfortable not knowing exactly where I'm going, and even feeling a little lost. I don't think about going from A to Z. I think about going from A to *B*. As long as I keep focusing on the next step, and keep moving forward, I know I will keep getting closer to success—in whatever form it takes.

## WHAT YOU DO IS WHO YOU ARE

Some people think it's okay to treat people poorly in the business world because, after all, it's just "business."

But I'm not one of them.

I don't split myself into two people. *There isn't one "business" Joy and one "mom" Joy. There is only one Joy, and everything I do comes from the same place—from my heart.*

I nearly lost my Miracle Mop to people who did unethical things. But I was able to push back and win the battle precisely because I conducted myself in a way that was fair and just—that's the way I try to act in *all* aspects of my life. It's what gives me the power to keep pushing forward.

Don't think in terms of "balancing" your business with the rest of your life. Figure out how it can all mesh together, so that all of your passion and principles in life flow naturally through all aspects of everything you do.

Do not split yourself into two people! Don't think, "This isn't who I am, it's just what I do."

What we do *is* who we are.

So do the right thing in all aspects of your life, and you will have all of the power on your side.

## YOU SPEAK UP FOR YOU

All of our voices matter. All of our voices can make a huge difference. But that can only happen if we make our voices heard—and we are the best ones to speak up for ourselves.

Some people don't want to speak up, or offer their opinion—even on matters that are crucially vital to them—because they're afraid of being judged or shamed or embarrassed. But none of those are good enough reasons not to speak up.

I stood up to my father after he smashed my chocolate snaps, and that made a difference in the way he treated me. Then I spoke up for myself to the buyer from Kmart, and to Dan at QVC, and to Eddie in the hotel room, and then to the judge in the courtroom. Believe me, I was scared each time, but I didn't let that stop me from speaking up. And when I did, it made a difference. In fact, it made *all* the difference.

Because if I didn't speak up for myself, no one else would have.

And besides, *there isn't anyone better in the world to speak up for us than ourselves. We are our own best advocates, our own best champions.* If we're fighting for something that is right and just and meaningful, then speaking up for ourselves can change our lives.

It can even change the world.

## DON'T BE AFRAID TO LEAN
## ON YOUR FAMILY

Don't mix business with family—everybody knows that, right? If you mix business with family, things can get *really* messy.

Well, the messy part is true. But I believe we should lean on our families anyway.

I wouldn't have been able to make the Miracle Mop if my father Rudy hadn't let me work out of his shop. And I wouldn't have been able to make 60,000 of them if I hadn't leaned on my family for help—and if the men and women from the church hadn't leaned on their families, too. And my children? They were always there for me when I needed them to pitch in.

Keeping my dreams and goals intertwined with the dreams and goals of my family has allowed us to stay together in some form for a long, long time. And, messy as it might have been, having my family with me on my journey has been one of the great blessings of my life.

*We should look at our families as an incredible resource that's right at our fingertips, and not be afraid to lean on them when our backs are against the wall.*

Believe me, it's worth getting a little messy to have your family with you on your journey.

## THERE ARE NO EXPERTS

There's a myth about successful people. The myth is that, because they have been doing something for a long time, and have been successful at it, they know exactly what can and cannot be done in their field.

That's simply not true.

You will meet people who know more about a particular field than you. Listen to them. Learn from them. But don't assume they know everything. Because, in truth, there are no experts.

An expert is only an expert until a better idea comes along, and that idea can come from anyone. Including you. I was told I shouldn't host the infomercial for the Miracle Mop because "women don't listen to women." That's what the experts said. But I persisted, and I made the infomercial, and I proved them wrong.

Sometimes, it's hard to trust your own instincts when someone you respect disagrees with you. I'll let you in on a secret little thing I do to keep reminding myself that there are no experts. If I'm in a meeting, and an "expert" tears into one of my ideas and tells me why it can't be done, I always say to myself, "This guy is an idiot."

I don't say that to be mean. I really don't. I say it because it helps me push through the criticism. It gives me the *fuel* I need to keep going.

Don't give anyone the power to be the ultimate decider of the worth of your idea. That you must keep for yourself. The experts may tell you you're wasting your time. If they do, just say, "This guy's an idiot."

Just don't say it out loud.

## ALWAYS TRY TO CIRCLE BACK

When I hired my ex-husband Tony to work for me, some people thought I was out of my mind. But I didn't see it that way. Just because Tony and I didn't work out as husband and wife didn't mean our relationship couldn't continue in a new incarnation. And in fact that's what happened—we became friends and colleagues.

It's easy to shut the door on a relationship that isn't working, but sometimes we're too quick to do that. Sometimes, it's worth circling back and taking another look. It's worth staying open to the relationship taking on a new and different form. This is true of spouses, friends, colleagues, business partners, next-door neighbors, whoever.

There might be a way to change the relationship, so we can keep a good person in our lives.

*In business and in life, I believe it's important for us to allow ourselves to circle back, to see if a relationship might work in a new incarnation.* That may not always be possible, but if it is, I believe it's worth a try.

## FAILURE FILLS YOUR BASKET

In life, every single experience we have is something we can learn from. And that is especially true of failure.

I look at failure as the chance to fill up my basket with resources. *All the hard lessons I learn by failing make me stronger and leave me better prepared to handle the next obstacle.*

Some people are so afraid of failing they will avoid all challenges and risks and confrontations. They think about the downside of what could happen, and that's enough to scare them away from even getting started.

But the downside can actually be an upside. The most successful people in life learn from everything that happens to them, even the really bad, painful things. They learn from their mistakes and they use these experiences as fuel to push them forward.

Failure fills up our baskets with resources, and makes us stronger and more resilient as we face whatever incredible challenge comes next.

## LIFE IS NOT A LOTTERY

Despite what some people might think, there isn't some magical, life-transforming prize waiting for us when we succeed. People sometimes believe that "success" means you figured out a way to live a life that is easy and free of worry. But that's not how it works. Because success isn't an end point—it's only the beginning.

Before I made the move from QVC to HSN, I had to define what success meant to me. And it didn't mean money, or status, or fame. It didn't mean being able to retire and never work again. Ultimately, for me, success was getting to do *more* of what I love to do.

You'll hear people say, "Oh, this is just my job, but what I'm really passionate about is this other thing." But what if we flipped that around?

Identify the thing you can't wait to get out of bed in the morning to do. The thing that really *ignites* you. Then, think about how you can achieve sustainable success doing it. If that sounds idealistic to you, you're probably right. I'm not saying it's an easy thing to do. But don't let that stop you from imagining a bigger, braver, and better life for yourself. I didn't let it stop me.

*The only definition of success that should matter to you is your own.*

## PRODUCT IS KING

A lot of factors can go into having a successful product—marketing, packaging, celebrity endorsements—but none of them matter unless the product itself *is a truly great product.*

In the world of commerce, you need to be sure the core of your business is solid. You need to make sure what you're offering the world is exceptional, innovative, and meaningful to people's lives. If it is, people will find you. It doesn't matter who you are, or where you came from—people will line up for what you're selling if it's a truly great product.

The same is true in life. We need to be sure that the core of who we are is authentic and solid, no matter what we choose to do in life. We could end up rich and living in a big house with a swimming pool and tennis courts—but unless the core of who we are is authentically, consistently great, all that glitter and gloss won't make us happy. So don't focus on fancy wrapping or empty packaging.

*Focus on the product—the core of who you are.*

## YOU ARE NEVER ABOVE IT ALL

Being successful doesn't mean we magically float to a place that is different and separate from our lives. The last thing we want to do is float away from everything that made us successful in the first place. There's no such thing as being "too successful" to work hard, stay close with people, and pay attention to details.

When I had my first success, I didn't suddenly change the way I work. And when someone made a movie based on my life, I didn't let that make me feel more important than the work I do. I was the same Joy on the red carpet of my movie premiere as I was doing mop demonstrations at Kmart.

Some people chase success because they don't want to take care of the nitty-gritty of their business. They're happy to delegate that work to someone else. But for me, the work that I do is all about the nitty-gritty. I make it a priority to be involved in *all* the details with everything I do.

I don't measure success in terms of how much work I can have other people handle for me. *Success for me is staying in your life, not above it.*

So let's follow our dreams and let them take us as far as they can, to places we never even imagined—even the Oscars! But when we get there, let's keep finding the joy in the beautiful nuts and bolts of our lives.

## JUST DON'T STOP

Ninety-nine percent of the time, when people don't succeed, it's because, for some reason, they stopped along the way. They just stopped. Maybe they didn't see the path. Maybe they took a no as a no. Maybe they thought they'd never reach the finish line.

But if there is no path, make another one. If you get a no, fight until it's a yes. If you can't see the finish line, focus on the next step.

*In life, there is always a way to keep going. No matter the setback or obstacle, there is always a solution, always a way forward.* In life, we're never "done"—there is always more to explore, more to conquer, more paths that will lead us to true happiness and joy.

As long as we just don't stop.

And in the case of this book, when I say don't stop, I really mean it. So just keep going—even after it looks like the book has ended. You'll find a collection of my favorite inspirational quotes, which I hope will move you as much as they move me. And you'll also find a way to reach out to me with your own ideas and insights.

And then, even after that, keep going.

Because a bit further on, tucked away in a secret place, you'll find a special message.

The message is *me* talking directly to *you* whenever you need me the most. It's me letting you know that you are going to live a joyful life each and every day. That together, you and I will make it happen.

So don't stop. Just keep going.

# ACKNOWLEDGMENTS

First and foremost, I'd like to thank my three amazing children. Christie, Bobby, and Jackie: you are my strength and my inspiration, more so than you could ever know. You are the reason this book exists. If it weren't for you, I may never have realized how much I've learned over my life, and how we might help others.

A deep and special thank you to my coauthor, Alex. I've said it before and I'll say it again—everything happens for a reason. Fate was smiling on us the day that you walked into my life. You have the talent and heart and soul of ten men, ten times over. Together we built that rocket ship, didn't we? With many more to come.

To my literary manager, the talented and tireless Heather Rizzo, thank you. You are the light bright person that turned this book from a spark of an idea into a full-blown force. And, in the process, we carved a brave new path together. The same is true for my publisher, Jonathan Karp, my editor, Christine Pride, and all of the talented people at Simon & Schuster. A note, and very special thanks, to the visionary Scott Koondel for bringing us all together.

And to all of my family and friends with whom I have had the pleasure of working throughout my career: thank you for believing in the power of new ideas, and for helping time and again to turn our collective dreams into reality. For that, I owe to you more than words can describe. You are my wings, and together we fly. A loving thank you to Tony Curto.

Finally, to you, the customer. Thank you for accepting me into your home for the past twenty-five years, and for trusting in me as we have taken this beautiful journey together. As I've known from the very beginning, and as I remind myself every day, you are always the smartest person in the room, and you have in your hands the power to change the world. Don't ever forget that.

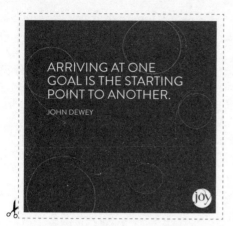

ARRIVING AT ONE
GOAL IS THE STARTING
POINT TO ANOTHER.

JOHN DEWEY

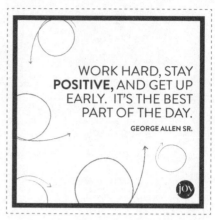

WORK HARD, STAY
**POSITIVE,** AND GET UP
EARLY. IT'S THE BEST
PART OF THE DAY.

**GEORGE ALLEN SR.**

A GOOD LAUGH IS
SUNSHINE IN A HOUSE.

WILLIAM MAKEPEACE THACKERAY

ALWAYS BELIEVE THAT
SOMETHING WONDERFUL
IS ABOUT TO HAPPEN.

SUKHRAJ S. DHILLON

DO WHAT YOU CAN
WITH WHAT YOU HAVE,
WHEREVER YOU ARE.

THEODORE ROOSEVELT

LIVE EACH DAY
AS IF YOUR LIFE
HAD **JUST** BEGUN.

JOHANN WOLFGANG VON GOETHE

DO SOMETHING
**WONDERFUL,**
PEOPLE MAY IMITATE IT.

ALBERT SCHWEITZER

FAITH IS TAKING
THE FIRST STEP
EVEN WHEN YOU
DON'T SEE THE
WHOLE STAIRCASE.

MARTIN LUTHER KING JR.

WORK HARD,
BE KIND,
AND **AMAZING THINGS**
WILL HAPPEN.

CONAN O'BRIEN

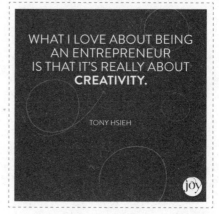

WHAT I LOVE ABOUT BEING
AN ENTREPRENEUR
IS THAT IT'S REALLY ABOUT
**CREATIVITY.**

TONY HSIEH

GIVE EVERY DAY THE
CHANCE TO BECOME
THE **MOST BEAUTIFUL**
DAY OF YOUR LIFE.

MARK TWAIN

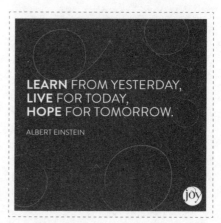

**LEARN** FROM YESTERDAY,
**LIVE** FOR TODAY,
**HOPE** FOR TOMORROW.

ALBERT EINSTEIN

TO BE SUCCESSFUL,
THE FIRST THING TO DO
IS **FALL IN LOVE**
WITH YOUR WORK.

SISTER MARY LAURETTA

THE BEST PREPARATION
FOR TOMORROW
IS DOING YOUR BEST
TODAY.

H. JACKSON BROWN JR.

**HAPPINESS**
OFTEN SNEAKS IN THROUGH
A DOOR YOU DIDN'T KNOW
YOU LEFT OPEN.

JOHN BARRYMORE

BEING **HAPPY**
NEVER GOES OUT OF STYLE.

LILY PULITZER

NURTURE YOUR MIND
WITH **GREAT THOUGHTS.**

BENJAMIN DISRAELI

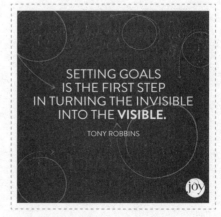

SETTING GOALS
IS THE FIRST STEP
IN TURNING THE INVISIBLE
INTO THE **VISIBLE.**

TONY ROBBINS

YOU CAN, YOU SHOULD, AND IF YOU'RE BRAVE ENOUGH TO START, YOU **WILL.**

STEPHEN KING

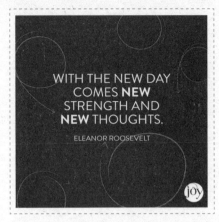

WITH THE NEW DAY COMES **NEW** STRENGTH AND **NEW** THOUGHTS.

ELEANOR ROOSEVELT

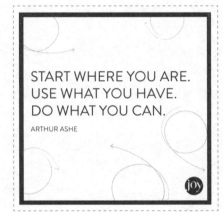

START WHERE YOU ARE. USE WHAT YOU HAVE. DO WHAT YOU CAN.

ARTHUR ASHE

I DO NOT TRY TO DANCE BETTER THAN ANYONE ELSE. I ONLY TRY TO DANCE BETTER THAN MYSELF.

MIKHAIL BARYSHNIKOV

THE REAL OPPORTUNITY FOR SUCCESS LIES **WITHIN** THE PERSON AND NOT IN THE JOB.

ZIG ZIGLAR

IN ORDER TO SUCCEED, WE MUST FIRST BELIEVE THAT WE CAN.

NIKOS KAZANTZAKIS

THE MERE FACT
OF BEING ABLE
TO CALL YOUR JOB
YOUR PASSION IS
SUCCESS IN MY EYES.

ALICIA VIKANDER

WHEN YOU HAVE A DREAM,
YOU'VE GOT TO **GRAB IT**
AND NEVER LET GO.

CAROL BURNETT

WHEN I BELIEVE IN
SOMETHING, I'M LIKE
A DOG WITH A BONE.

MELISSA McCARTHY

BELIEVE YOU CAN
AND
YOU'RE HALFWAY THERE.

THEODORE ROOSEVELT

IF NOT US, WHO?
IF NOW NOW, WHEN?

JOHN F. KENNEDY

THERE'S A MILLION THINGS
I HAVEN'T DONE,
BUT **JUST YOU WAIT.**

*HAMILTON:*
AN AMERICAN MUSICAL

DO NOT GO WHERE
THE PATH MAY LEAD.
GO INSTEAD WHERE
THERE IS NO PATH
AND **LEAVE A TRAIL.**

RALPH WALDO EMERSON

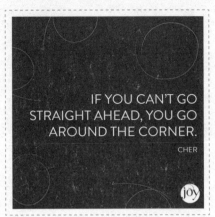

IF YOU CAN'T GO
STRAIGHT AHEAD, YOU GO
AROUND THE CORNER.

CHER

THE SECRET
OF GETTING AHEAD
IS **GETTING STARTED.**

MARK TWAIN

NOTHING IS IMPOSSIBLE.
THE WORD ITSELF SAYS
**"I'M POSSIBLE."**

AUDREY HEPBURN

TRIUMPH IS JUST
TRY WITH A LITTLE
**UMPH** ADDED TO IT.

UNKNOWN

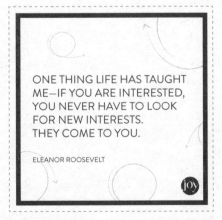

ONE THING LIFE HAS TAUGHT
ME—IF YOU ARE INTERESTED,
YOU NEVER HAVE TO LOOK
FOR NEW INTERESTS.
THEY COME TO YOU.

ELEANOR ROOSEVELT

I DWELL IN
**POSSIBILITY.**

EMILY DICKINSON

YOU CAN'T BUILD
A REPUTATION ON
WHAT YOU'RE
GOING TO DO.

HENRY FORD

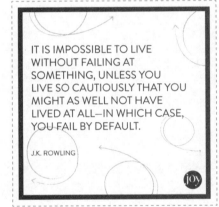

IT IS IMPOSSIBLE TO LIVE
WITHOUT FAILING AT
SOMETHING, UNLESS YOU
LIVE SO CAUTIOUSLY THAT YOU
MIGHT AS WELL NOT HAVE
LIVED AT ALL—IN WHICH CASE,
YOU FAIL BY DEFAULT.

J.K. ROWLING

YOU ARE NEVER TOO OLD
TO SET ANOTHER GOAL OR
TO DREAM A NEW DREAM.

C.S. LEWIS

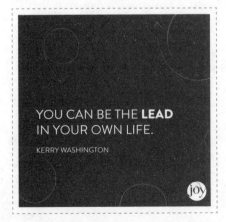

YOU CAN BE THE **LEAD**
IN YOUR OWN LIFE.

KERRY WASHINGTON

I WAS SMART ENOUGH
TO GO THROUGH ANY
DOOR THAT OPENED.

JOAN RIVERS

THE BIGGEST ADVENTURE
YOU CAN TAKE IS TO
LIVE THE LIFE OF
YOUR DREAMS.

OPRAH WINFREY

ALWAYS BEAR
IN MIND THAT YOUR OWN
RESOLUTION TO SUCCEED
IS MORE IMPORTANT THAN
ANY OTHER ONE THING.

ABRAHAM LINCOLN

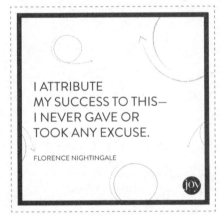

I ATTRIBUTE
MY SUCCESS TO THIS—
I NEVER GAVE OR
TOOK ANY EXCUSE.

FLORENCE NIGHTINGALE

IT'S NOT WHAT
OTHER PEOPLE BELIEVE
YOU CAN DO, IT'S
WHAT **YOU BELIEVE.**

GAIL DEVERS

MAKE EACH DAY
YOUR MASTERPIECE.

JOHN WOODEN

YOU HAD
THE **POWER**
ALL ALONG
MY DEAR.

GLINDA THE GOOD WITCH

Tear me out and use me as a label!

My Ideas for Joy
PO Box 649
Smithtown, NY 11787

*Dear Joy:*

_____

_____

_____

_____

_____

_____

_____

_____

_____

_____

_____

_____

_____

_____

_____

_____

_____

_____

*To You:*

*Hello again! I'm happy you made it here. I want to share something with you.*

*It's something I used to tell my children whenever they were down in the dumps, and whenever I was down there, too.*

*On the gloomiest days, I'd say, "Look at that! Can you see it? The sun's coming out through the clouds."*

*I still say that all the time. "Just look, the sun's coming, soon you'll see it."*

*No matter how bad things get for you, please know this—I've been there. If your mind is tired and your heart is sad and you feel like you just can't cope anymore, I've been there, too. I know what it's like to feel there's no way forward.*

*But I'm okay now. I made it through okay, and you will, too. You will be more than okay—you'll be great.*

*Because you are, and you always will be, your own brilliant creation.*

*No one in history has ever done what you've done so far, or what you will do when you put down this book and get back to being the beautiful invention you are.*

*We all have the power to summon the singleness of purpose and the strength of heart to live the brave, creative lives we want to live. The power is in me, and it's in you, too.*

*If you feel like no one believes in you, you are wrong. Because I believe in you. I believe in you because I am you. I know what you're capable of, and I believe in the magic of what you will create going forward.*

*And you should know that I am not wrong about this.*

*But it's not so important that I believe in you.*

*What's really important is that you believe in yourself.*

*You have to find that special thing that makes you believe in you.*

*But how can you do that when everything's broken and nothing is working and all hope seems lost?*

*Follow these steps:*

1. *Take a deep breath. Smell the air. Then do it again.*
2. *Next, do something that makes you smile. Go to a movie. Plant your garden. Make a list of the positives in your life. Find the person who always makes you laugh. Do anything. As long as it genuinely makes you smile.*
3. *Then, get to work. Realize this isn't the end of the world. Think hard about what's happening and figure out your next step. Figure out the way forward, one step at a time.*

*Because no matter how bad things get, there is always a way forward. Believe me, I know. I was there. And I'm okay. And you will be okay, too.*

*Our paths are all different, and yours is unique to you, and it is beautiful.*

*Because the truth is, we don't follow our paths.*

*We create them.*

*All of the power and courage and artistry to create a joyful life for yourself is already in you. You have everything you need to be the inventor of you. But you must believe that you are an amazing, original, brilliant inventor. You must believe that your ideas are valid and special and meaningful.*

*I believe in you and your ideas, and you must believe in them, too.*

*Feel me putting my arms around you and saying, "Believe in yourself."*

*And look at that. Can you see it? The sun's coming out through the clouds.*

*So be brave. Be creative. Take wing.* Soar.

*Your idea for you is beautiful, and I can't wait to see what you will make.*

*With much love,*

*Joy*

# ABOUT THE AUTHOR

JOY MANGANO is an inventor, entrepreneur, business executive, and TV personality with more than 100 patents and trademarks to her name. More importantly, Joy is a proud mother of three, and a proud grandmother of two. Joy continues to live in Long Island, New York, where she started her business, and where it is still headquartered today. *Inventing Joy* is Joy's first published work, and the capstone to an incomparable career. But, if you ask her, she'll most likely tell you that she's just getting warmed up.